ST BASIL THE GREAT

On the Human Condition

ST VLADIMIR'S SEMINARY PRESS
Popular Patristics Series

Series Editor
JOHN BEHR

ST BASIL THE GREAT

On the
*H*uman Condition

Translation and
Introduction by

NONNA VERNA HARRISON

ST VLADIMIR'S SEMINARY PRESS
CRESTWOOD, NEW YORK
2005

Library of Congress Cataloging-in-Publication Data

Basil, Saint, Bishop of Caesarea, ca. 329–379.
   [Selections. English. 2005]
   On the human condition / St. Basil the Great ; translation and introduction by
Nonna Verna Harrison.
      p.   cm. — (St. Vladimir's Seminary Press "popular patristics" series)
   Includes bibliographical references.
   ISBN 0–88141–294–5 (alk. paper)
    1. Man (Christian theology)—Sermons.   2. Philosophical anthropology—
Sermons.   3. Sermons, Early Christian.   I. Harrison, Verna E. F.   II. Title.
III. Series.

BR65.B33E6 2005
233—dc22

2005005588

For my students.

Contents

Preface

The idea for this book originated in the spring semester of 1993, when I was teaching at St Vladimir's Seminary. Paisius Whitesides, a bright and creative student with a gift for languages, asked me to work with him on reading Patristic Greek. Together we worked through part of the *Sources chrétiennes* edition of St Basil's two homilies on the human creation accounts. Each of us translated the same passage each week, and then we discussed it. I appreciated his labor, his enthusiasm and his insights. Since these texts are of considerable interest and had not previously been translated into English, Ted Bazil, the managing editor of St Vladimir's Seminary Press, suggested I continue this work and expand it into a book, whose title he supplied. Because of my many other responsibilities, this plan has taken a long time to come to fruition. I appreciate Ted's great patience and encouragement and that of Fr John Behr, who is now the series editor.

A classically trained friend in California, Matthew P. Johnson, translated the Latin version of the *Homily Explaining that God is Not the Cause of Evil* from the Migne edition, since this text had not yet been translated into English either. While his version proved helpful and I am thankful for the hard work he devoted to it, I found that the Latin was a paraphrase of the original Greek, which I have translated myself into the same contemporary English style used in the rest of this volume. I was also able to consult a good recent French translation of this homily by Marie-Claude Rosset. For the other texts I could consult previous English renderings. However, all the material in this book is my responsibility, particularly any errors it contains.

The texts translated here provide a valuable introduction to some major themes in Greek Patristic anthropology and are less speculative than the better-known works of Basil's brother, St Gregory of Nyssa. I would like to thank my students at St Joseph of Arimathea College in Berkeley, Saint Paul University in Ottawa, the Institute for Orthodox Christian Studies in Cambridge, England, and Saint Paul School of Theology in Kansas City, Missouri, for reading manuscripts of these translations with me, together with those to whom James Skedros taught this material at the Graduate Theological Union in Berkeley. This volume is dedicated to them and to all other students who may learn from it.

Sr Nonna Verna Harrison
March 29, 2004

Introduction

Born in 329 or 330, the author of the texts translated in this small book is the oldest of the three Cappadocian fathers, who were linked by ties of family, friendship, and education and who were major figures in the fourth-century flowering of Greek Christian literature, culture, spirituality, and theology. He is known in the Orthodox world as St Basil the Great, Archbishop of Caesarea in Cappadocia. St Gregory the Theologian, from Nazianzus, was his friend and fellow student, and St Gregory of Nyssa was his younger brother. These men came from a mountainous region of what is now central Turkey and belonged to two if its aristocratic families, each remarkable for producing several saints. There were Cappadocian mothers as well as fathers. Basil's grandmother St Macrina the Elder and his older sister St Macrina the Younger were instrumental in leading their family into lives of holiness, and Gregory Nazianzen's mother, St Nonna, played a similar role in her family.

The three Cappadocian theologians were steeped in the heritage of classical Greek literature and philosophy and brought its riches into their work as Christian pastors and teachers, thinkers, and writers. Basil and Gregory Nazianzen studied together for at least five years in Athens, which in the fourth century A.D. was a university town, an ancient and distinguished center of classical learning, rather as Oxford or Cambridge is today. There they learned the art of rhetoric, one of the primary forms of cultural expression in the

Late Antique Mediterranean world. Its practice included the composition of finely wrought artistic prose and also skill in the public speaking that was used in law courts and public administration but was a popular performing art as well. Both Cappadocians became master rhetoricians, though Gregory Nazianzen's writings exhibit more exuberance and poetic brilliance. Basil's prose is characterized by balance and sobriety, by clarity and relative simplicity.

Following his studies, Basil made a tour of monastic settlements in Egypt and the Middle East, and then returned to Cappadocia. He founded a men's ascetic community on lands owned by his family at Annesi, across the river Iris from where his sister Macrina had already turned their home into a women's community. Basil went on to found or organize ascetic communities for men and women across Cappadocia, for which he wrote extensive instructions. He favored the cenobitic way of life as opposed to the less-structured eremitical and semi-eremitical patterns that were also current in his time, though these continued to be practiced even among his friends and family. Significantly, he integrated ascetic groups into the life of the Christian community as a whole, and he harnessed their energies to the tasks of caring for the sick and poor and educating the young. Of course, they also continued to focus on prayer and manual labor to support themselves and each other. His gifts of insight and leadership in community life made him one of the leading founders of Eastern Christian monasticism. His ascetical writings were soon translated into Latin and subsequently recommended by St Benedict, so they were influential in the West too, throughout the Middle Ages and beyond.

After a few years in Annesi, Basil went to Caesarea, the capital of Cappadocia, where he was ordained priest. He assisted the bishop in political negotiations and theological controversy and built charitable institutions to care for the hungry and ill during a severe famine. He became bishop of Caesarea himself in 370, a post he held until his death, probably on January 1, 379. These were years of intense activity, though he struggled repeatedly with poor health. As an ecclesiastical statesman he corresponded with many civic, cultural and church leaders throughout the empire. He wrote theological treatises advocating the doctrine of the Trinity and led the Homoiousian party in its reconciliation with Athanasius' strict Nicene contingent, as they made a common front against Arians and neo-Arians. The two Gregorys collaborated in this task, and in 381 they took part in the Council of Constantinople, which ratified Basil's position, vindicating the Creed of Nicea and adding an article that clearly affirmed the divine status of the Holy Spirit, about which he had written a major treatise.

Besides encouraging social justice on behalf of the poor, Basil took a great interest in personal morality and spirituality. His homilies on virtues and vices show considerable philosophical learning and psychological insight. One of these, directed against anger, is translated here. His writings also reveal him to be a contemplative, as Ann Keidel has shown,[1] a point often overlooked by scholars who are impressed with him as a man of action and contrast him with his brother Gregory of Nyssa, a renowned mystical theologian. Another of his major concerns is the interpretation of Scripture. At times, for example in some of his Psalm homilies, he employs the allegorical methods traditional among Greek-speaking Christians of his era. Like other ancient commentators, he understands Ps 45, the royal wedding hymn, as celebrating the marriage between Christ and the church. More often he focuses on the literal meanings of biblical texts with the aim of identifying the moral precepts they contain and discerning how to live by them with rigor and exactitude. He seeks always to live a serious Christian lifestyle in practice and to teach others to do likewise. All of these concerns lead him to take an interest in the theology of the human person, to which he returns throughout his career. He brings an inquiring mind educated in Scripture and Greek philosophy to the questions posed by the

[1] *"Hesychia,* Prayer and Transformation in Basil of Caesarea," *Studia Patristica* 34 (2001): 110–20.

human condition and addresses them with characteristic clarity, sobriety, and balance. The present book brings together some of his main writings on the subject.

The Texts Translated

The first two homilies included in this volume are clearly written together and comment on the human creation accounts in the first two chapters of Genesis, and they are preserved together in the manuscript tradition. There has been some question about their authorship, and specialists are not entirely agreed on this point. Late in his life Basil wrote a famous series of nine homilies *On the Six Days of Creation* that end just before discussing the creation of human beings in Gen 1.26–27, the point where the biblical narrative reaches a climax. Basil then promises to complete his task later, but was he really able to fulfill his pledge? Gregory of Nyssa subsequently wrote a major treatise *On the Creation of Humanity* that claims to complete the work his brother left unfinished. This could be taken as indicating that Basil did not actually write these two homilies, which begin with his statement that he is completing an earlier unfinished task himself. Yet Gregory's relationship with the older brother he calls his "father and teacher" is more complex than it appears on the surface. More than once he makes tacit but significant changes in Basil's teachings in the process of defending or completing his works.

Alexis Smets and Michel van Esbroeck, the editors of the *Sources chrétiennes* edition translated here, consider them to be Basil's homilies ten and eleven *On the Six Days of Creation.*[2] However, in the manuscript tradition, they are not preserved with the other nine. Most of the manuscripts do ascribe them to Basil, though a few ascribe them to Gregory of Nyssa, and some leave them anonymous. Clearly Gregory is not the author, since the theological anthropology

<hr>

[2] *Basile de Césarée: Sur l'origine de l'homme,* SC 160 (Paris: Cerf, 1970).

articulated in these homilies differs in some important matters of detail from the distinctive positions expressed in his authentic writings. In particular, unlike these homilies he does not distinguish between the divine image and likeness. On the other hand, they contain a number of close parallels to things Basil says elsewhere in his undisputed works, including some translated here. Scholars are largely agreed that the thought they express is that of Basil, which is why they belong in this volume.

The puzzling question, then, is why their style differs from that of his other writings in a way that will probably be obvious to careful readers of these translations. It is choppy and lacks the refinement and clear, balanced syntax of his usual rhetorical prose. Specialists have suggested two alternative explanations of this body of evidence. Some say Basil wrote the homilies at the end of his life and did not have time to edit them for publication before his death. Others say they were composed in Cappadocia after his death by a close disciple of his on the basis of his notes and manuscripts.[3] It is noteworthy how close these two positions actually are to each other.

The first of these homilies discusses the human creation account in Gen 1 while the second is about the account in Gen 2. All commentators on this biblical material have to address the issue of why these chapters provide two very different stories of how human beings were created. Today's biblical scholars generally rely on source criticism for an explanation, but this methodology was

---

[3]For clear summaries of scholarly arguments for and against their authenticity, see Smets and van Esbroeck, pp. 13–126, and Emmanuel Amand de Mendieta, "Les deux homélies sur la création de l'homme que les manuscrits attribuent à Basile de Césarée ou à Grégoire de Nysse: Le problème de leur rédaction," in *Zetesis: Album amicorum* [Festschrift for E. de Strycker] (Antwerp and Utrecht: Nederlandsche Boekhandel, 1973). Basil's biographer Philip Rousseau presented a lecture on these homilies at the Fourteenth International Conference on Patristic Studies at Oxford, 18–23 August 2003, entitled "Human Nature and Its Material Setting in Basil of Caesarea's Sermons on the Creation." He argued for their authenticity, analyzed the texts and read excerpts from his own draft translation. Unfortunately, he has not submitted this material for publication in *Studia Patristica*.

unavailable in the ancient world, where Jews and Christians all assumed that Moses wrote the whole narrative. Philo, Origen, and Gregory of Nyssa, each in a different way, believed that the two accounts name two fundamentally distinct phases in God's creative plan or activity. Basil does not subscribe to any of these "double creation" theories but states simply that Gen 1 describes *what* God created while Gen 2 tells *how* he did so. Basil also distinguishes between what God "made" in Gen 1, namely those aspects of the human creation that manifest the divine image, and what is "molded" in Gen 2, namely the human body, which enjoys the dignity of being fashioned by God's own hands.

Like the two homilies on the human creation, the third text in the book is translated into English here for the first time from *Patrologia Graeca* 31.329–354. The *Homily Explaining that God is Not the Cause of Evil* discusses, among other things, the account of the Fall in Gen 3. It is probably among Basil's earlier works and in all likelihood was written in Caesarea during the devastating famine mentioned above. In the context of his concern that the rich share their stores of money and food with the poor, Basil interprets the community's sufferings as God's wake up call to the city's inhabitants aimed at arousing their repentance. The homily's explanations of how natural disasters and human-made calamities express divine providence are very traditional in ancient Christianity, although many of the faithful today may find them at least in part unconvincing and prefer apophatic reserve in the face of questions about why God allows such things to happen. In this text Basil also seeks to explain why Adam and Eve chose to disobey God and eat the forbidden fruit in the first place, and further, why Satan who deceived them originally chose to sin.

The rest of the book provides new translations of works that complement the first three texts. The next three focus on the roles played by different human faculties in our experience, moral discipline, and spiritual praxis. The *Homily against Anger* (*Patrologia Graeca* 31.354–372) begins with vivid descriptions of the destructive consequences of anger run wild and proposes philosophical and spiritual exercises to help control it. It goes on to provide a philosophical analysis of the place of emotions in the structure of the human person and an account of how when rightly directed they fulfill necessary, positive functions in moral and spiritual life. The *Homily on the Words "Be Attentive to Yourself"* is a classic text in which Basil suggests various practical applications of his theological understanding of human identity. Stig Y. Rudberg has provided a good critical edition of this work,[4] which I have translated. The balance Basil recommends here between humility grounded in our creation from the earth and confidence based on the dignity of being created according to God's image is particularly noteworthy. *Letter 233*, translated from Yves Courtonne's edition of Basil's letters,[5] is one of many he wrote to his spiritual son, Gregory Nazianzen's cousin Amphilochius of Iconium, who often asked him about theological, spiritual, and pastoral issues. His questions elicited a number of Basil's important writings. This letter succinctly discusses the functions of the human mind, the activity for which God created it, and how it can be used for good, evil, or morally neutral purposes. It complements the discussion of emotions in the *Homily against Anger*.

Finally, we have included excerpts from the beginning of Basil's instructions to his ascetic communities, commonly known as the *Long Rules* or the *Great Asceticon* (*Patrologia Graeca* 31.906–934). Here he discusses the communal dimension of human identity, an issue of great contemporary interest and theological significance. He asserts that humans are created in such a way that they are naturally interrelated, social, and interdependent. So it is natural for them to love God, their creator and benefactor, and it is likewise natural for them to love their neighbors. Thus, in Basil's mind the conclusions

---

[4] *L'homélie de Basile de Césarée sur le mot 'Observe-toi toi-même': Édition critique du texte grec et étude sur la tradition manuscrite*, Acta Universitatis Stockholmiensis, Studia Graeca Stockholmiensia 2 (Stockholm: Almqvist & Wiksell, 1962), 23–37.

[5] *Saint Basile: Lettres*, 3 vols. (Paris: Les Belles Lettres, 1957–66), 3:39–41.

of philosophical anthropology support and harmoniously accord with the foremost commandments of the Gospel.

The Image and Likeness of God

The rest of this introduction will attempt to summarize some of the main anthropological themes discussed in the translated texts. In this context it will also explain some specific issues of translation. The most fundamental theme, of course, is the image of God named in Gen 1.26–27, which from the New Testament onward emerged as the foundational concept in nearly all Christian reflection on what it is to be human and has played this role throughout the church's history. Basil and other Greek fathers characteristically distinguish between Christ, who is *the* Image of God *par excellence* (cf. Col 1.15), since in his divine nature he is of one essence with the Father and is thus perfectly like him, and the human person who is said in Gen 1 to be created *according to* God's image and likeness. The early Greek Christian theologians thus employ a technical term to refer to those aspects of humanity that manifest the divine image, namely *to kat' eikona*, which I have translated literally as "that which is according to the image." It is important to note that Basil avoids referring loosely to human beings as "the image of God," although scholars often use such language in discussing Christian anthropologies, including those of the fathers. Basil reserves this title for Christ. When other human persons share in the divine image—and the Cappadocians affirm in the strongest terms that they do—this occurs because Christ as divine Logos is the model according to which they are created, and they thus have the capacity to participate in him and imitate his incarnate life.

Basil makes three other distinctions that clarify his understanding of how human beings manifest the divine image. First, as noted above, he balances the dignity of the *imago Dei* with the lowliness of being created from the earth's dust, as noted in Gen 2. He teaches that if we are mindful of both contrasting aspects of our human creation, our sense of who we are is firmly grounded and we can guard against the temptations of arrogance and discouragement, both of which arise from a feeling that our underlying identity is unstable. Second, he explicitly locates the divine image, and with it the core of human identity, in the rational aspect of the soul, not in the body. He says that the soul is what each of us *is* as a human being, our body properly belongs to each of us, but material possessions do not truly belong to us. However, he discusses at length the wonder and dignity of the body, which has been created as a fitting vehicle for that which bears God's image. Its beauty and ingenious structure make it a masterpiece of divine craftsmanship. Third, he distinguishes between that which is according to the image, the rationality and free choice that humans always have, and that which is according to the likeness, the deiform virtues that we can acquire through participation in Christ by using our freedom to cooperate with the Holy Spirit. Basil notes that God has honored humans by enabling them to become fashioners of the divine likeness within themselves.

Like the biblical text he is interpreting, Basil also links the divine image with human authority over the earth and its creatures. He gives several picturesque examples of how people can use ingenuity made possible by their rational faculties to trap and humiliate animals. These passages may prove disturbing to many readers today, since we live in an age when numerous species are endangered or have become extinct because of human exploitation or encroachment on their habitats. In our time it is essential to understand that the commandments of love for God and neighbor extend to include love for the natural world in which we live. Because we bear God's image we are called to nurture and protect the earth and its creatures. Our authority is best understood as a royal priesthood whose vocation is to offer the world and everything in it to God and bestow God's blessing on the world and everything in it. To put Basil's discussion of animals in perspective, it helps to understand that conditions were very different in his time. Hunters and fishermen could use their skills and technologies to overcome wild animals, but it was a perilous endeavor, and the animals still had a fair chance to win. Basil had a brother named Naucratius who died as a young man in a hunting or fishing accident. Moreover, Basil makes clear that the most important way humans are called to exercise authority over the animals is by controlling the beasts within oneself, that is, the passions. He asks what human dignity can be found in a man who cages and tames a lion but is ruled by his own anger so that he roars and claws his prey like a wild beast. Basil also notes that although God has invited humankind to multiply and fill the earth, the most important kinds of increase are our own spiritual growth and the growth of the church community throughout the world.

The purpose of human existence and participation in the divine image is fulfilled in knowledge and vision of God, likeness to God and union with him. Basil describes this in chapter 9 of his treatise *On the Holy Spirit*, a famous passage that is worth quoting at length.

> The Spirit's closeness to the soul does not occur through an approach of place. For how could one come near in a bodily manner to the incorporeal? It occurs through separation from the passions, which arise in the soul following friendship toward the flesh and alienate it from closeness to God. So then, being purified from the ugliness smeared on through evil and returning to the beauty of [human] nature and as it were through purity restoring to the royal image its ancient form is the only manner of approaching the Paraclete. And he, like a sun joining itself to a purified eye, will show you in himself the image of the invisible. And in the blessed vision of the Image you will see the ineffable beauty of the Archetype.[6] Through the Spirit, hearts are lifted up, the weak are led by the hand, those making progress are perfected. It is he who, shining on those purified from every

[6]By "Image" here, Basil refers to the Son, and by "Archetype" to the Father.

stain, through communion with himself shows them forth as spiritual. And just as limpid and transparent bodies, when the sun's ray falls upon them, themselves become radiant and shine with another ray from themselves, so the Spirit-bearing souls illumined by the Spirit themselves become spiritual and send forth the grace to others. From this comes foreknowledge of future events, understanding of mysteries, comprehension of hidden things, distribution of gifts, heavenly citizenship, dancing with angels, joy without end, abiding in God, likeness to God, and the summit of desires, becoming god.[7]

According to Basil, the use of the plural, "Let us make," in Gen 1.26 shows that the persons of the Trinity took counsel among themselves about creating the human being. Basil explains that this supports the Nicene faith by identifying the Son and Spirit as co-creators with the Father. Moreover, in his understanding it strongly affirms the dignity of humankind, disclosing it as a masterpiece of divine craftsmanship. Yet perhaps this point has a further implication as well. If our creation according to the divine image emerges from the shared deliberation and activity of the divine persons, is not our core human identity rooted in the mutual relationship, love, and communion that constitute the life of the Trinity itself? For the most part the fathers, including Basil, understand the human *imago Dei* primarily in Christological terms. Yet, I would suggest, the seeds of a Trinitarian understanding are present in their writings as well, though such Trinitarian anthropologies do not come to full flower until the twentieth and twenty-first centuries. This is a topic that lies outside the scope of our brief introduction and calls for further investigation. My point here is that the Trinitarian understanding of the "Let us make" that occurs in Basil's first

[7]Benoît Pruche, ed., *Basile de Césarée: Sur le Saint-Esprit*, Sources chrétiennes 17 bis, 2nd edition revised and augmented (Paris: Cerf, 2002), 326–28, my translation.

homily on the human creation, at greater length near the end of his ninth homily *On the Six Days of Creation*, and in many other patristic texts, can provide one of the starting points for such a study.

The Character and Activities of the Human Soul

In the ancient world, the soul is understood as engaging in a broader range of activities than are sometimes ascribed to it today. It gives life to the body, so that without a soul a body becomes a cadaver. It also is the locus of human mental and emotional faculties including reason, free choice and conscience, fear and desire, sorrow and joy. Plato articulated a tripartite model of the soul that became standard in the popular philosophy current in Late Antiquity and then also in much of the Eastern Christian tradition of spiritual psychology. One of the best brief descriptions of these psychological terms can be found in the glossary at the end of each volume of the English translation of the *Philokalia*.[8] Basil and the other Cappadocians presuppose and employ this tripartite model, and several texts in this book refer to it, so we will describe it in some detail. It is important to note that it names distinct activities of the human person that interact in various ways, not separate, self-enclosed, static entities that form components of the self. What follows is a somewhat simplified overview of this psychology as it appears in Basil's writings.

The first or highest of the three parts is reason, mind, or intellect,[9] though this is understood as something greater, deeper, and broader than the "reasoning brain" emphasized today. Its activities include cognition and reasoning but also moral insight and deliberation, and freedom of choice. The intellect perceives the material world through the senses and organizes and evaluates these perceptions.

[8]For example, G. E. H. Palmer, Philip Sherrard and Kallistos Ware, trans. *The Philokalia, Volume I* (London: Faber and Faber, 1979), 357–67.

[9]I am simplifying by using these terms interchangeably here.

Yet its highest and most important function is to perceive spiritual realities including other people as spiritual beings, angels, and ultimately God, as Basil explains in the text from *On the Holy Spirit,* 9, quoted above. In *Letter 233* he explains succinctly how the mind can be used for good, evil, or morally neutral purposes, depending where it focuses its attention.

In a mature, well balanced human life, our intellect is supposed to discern, receive, and obey the will of God and to guide and bring order to the other two faculties of the soul, which are understood as including the instinctive and emotional impulses and drives. Like the mind, both of these nonrational faculties can be used for good or evil purposes, depending in which directions they turn and move. One of these faculties is desire, which seeks to move a person toward various things or persons, or draw them toward the self. Desire is easily misdirected when obsessively focused on the flesh or material possessions, but it also serves as the necessary driving force in love for God and love for neighbor.

The other nonrational faculty is called *thumos* in Greek, a word that is difficult to translate. It is sometimes rendered as "emotion," which is too broad and vague; sometimes as "spirit," which could be confused with *pneuma,* a word meaning something entirely different; or "passion," which again invites confusion with something different, namely *pathos.* The translators of the *Philokalia* call it the "incensive faculty," a name that appears to have no meaning in contemporary English except as a technical term rendering *thumos.* This faculty complements desire in that it pushes things away from the self and sets limits on other impulses, one's own or those of other people. Plato and later writers influenced by Platonism including Christian fathers see well-ordered *thumos* as a useful ally to reason in curbing one's inordinate desires. Basil compares it to a loyal soldier who has left his weapons with his wise general, that is reason, and is ready to serve at his commander's bidding. *Thumos* is also the necessary driving force at work in virtues like perseverance, courage, self-restraint, rejection of evil, and struggle for justice. Yet *thumos* is most closely associated with anger, and in some contexts this is what it means, though clearly it has a broader range of meanings.

Sometimes it is translated as "anger," though I have used this to render another word that more specifically focuses on this meaning, *orge*. It has proved challenging to find appropriate but distinct renderings for *thumos* and *orge*, terms that play central roles in the *Homily against Anger*, where both are used frequently in somewhat technical ways, and their meanings at times overlap but are not identical. Perhaps one of the best English renderings of *thumos* is "assertiveness," especially when this is understood as distinct from aggression. But in this homily, where it sometimes means destructive anger and sometimes the faculty of soul that can be used in various ways for good or evil, I have chosen to call it "temper," or occasionally "bad temper." This is my attempt to encompass a range of meanings and connotations—the human faculty that can become good or bad temper, the strength achieved in tempering steel, and sometimes simply anger.

When a person's life is rightly ordered, all these impulses and drives work together harmoniously in serving virtue, guided by reason and obedient to God's will. However, this harmony, which existed in the original human state in paradise, has become disrupted in humankind's fallen condition. Our soul's faculties pull us in different directions and are often in conflict with each other. There can also be a conflict between soul and body in which the body functions as a heavy weight pulling us downward and away from God. Yet Basil is always mindful that the body and the emotional faculties are given us by our Creator for good purposes, and that the mind, too, can be sinfully misused. Thus the whole person either turns toward God, turns away from him in sin, or turns back toward him in repentance. When all the human faculties are again directed toward God, their original harmony is restored. Much of Basil's preaching aims to lead us toward this restoration.

Gender and Community

In the *First Discourse on the Origin of Humanity*, §18, there is an interesting discussion of the place of gender in human identity. Basil represents a woman in the audience as asking why women are bound by the strenuous moral imperatives that go with bearing the divine image, a responsibility she suggests is borne by men alone. Her question is based on a fine point in the interpretation of the Septuagint version of Gen 1.27 that does not translate easily into English. The verse reads, "and God made the human being according to his image." It contains the standard Greek word for the human being, *ho anthropos*, an inclusive term that contrasts with *ho aner*, which specifically means the male. The difficulty is that in Greek the definite article, translated "the," has grammatical gender, a usage with no direct equivalent in English. Basil's questioner asks why Gen 1.27 uses the masculine form, *ho*, instead of the feminine *he anthropos*. The latter is an unusual form in Patristic Greek but is sometimes used to refer precisely to a human person who happens to be female.[10] The closest English equivalent would perhaps be to mention a "human being" to whom the pronoun "she" then refers. In my translation, I have resorted to inserting [fem.] and [masc.] after the uses of "the" that are at issue.

Basil responds with a strong affirmation that men and women alike are fully human, that both are created according to God's image, and that between them "the natures are alike of equal honor, the virtues are equal, the struggles equal, the judgment alike." That is, both genders are called to the same life of faith, good works, holiness, and the divine likeness; both will encounter the same divine judgment in the next life, and their subsequent rewards and punishments will be based on their conduct, without discrimination due

[10]For examples, see my article, "Women, Human Identity and the Image of God: Antiochene Interpretations," *Journal of Early Christian Studies* 9 (2001): 205–49, at 210–11.

to other factors. This is because women are just as capable of faith, good works, and holiness as men are, regardless of their bodily differences and any weakness this involves. Basil gives examples of how women often surpass men in some of the strenuous bodily exercises practiced in the ascetic life, as well as in acts of compassion and charity. To understand his point, it helps to note that early Christian asceticism involved a level of physical training and endurance comparable to that found among professional athletes today. Basil concludes that the distinction between male and female is present only in the body, not in the soul. Elsewhere he adds that in the age to come the gender distinction will no longer be present in resurrected bodies either. Although this view may appear strange to some readers today who envisage profound spiritual differences between men and women, Basil's perspective is shared by the two Cappadocian Gregorys and many of the other Greek fathers.[11]

Another issue relevant to contemporary concerns is Basil's clear affirmation of the communal dimension of human identity. He discusses this at the beginning of the *Long Rules*, a work that advocates cenobitic forms of monastic life and criticizes the more eremitical forms. Echoing an ancient philosophical commonplace, in Question 3 he observes that "the human being is a tame and communal animal, and is neither solitary nor savage," and that "nothing is so proper to our nature as to share our lives with each other, and to need each other, and to love our own kind." Basil goes on to show how Christ's commandment of love builds on this natural aptitude. He then offers a profound meditation on the spiritual benefits of

[11]See Basil's *Homily on Psalm 145*, PG 29:492C: "For there is no male or female in the resurrection, but there is one certain life and it is of one kind, since those dwelling in the land of the living are well pleasing to their Master." For the theological meaning and cultural context of this statement and many related patristic texts, see my articles, Verna E. F. Harrison, "Male and Female in Cappadocian Theology," *Journal of Theological Studies*, n.s. 41 (1990): 441–71; and Nonna Verna Harrison, "Women, Human Identity, and the Image of God: Antiochene Interpretations," *Journal of Early Christian Studies* 9 (2001): 205–249.

community life. In practice many of his counsels apply to all Christians, including those called to a more solitary form of monasticism. In this discussion he does not connect his ideas about human community with the themes of the image of God and the Trinity but develops them in a Christological context. Many contemporary theologians would make such connections, though; Basil's understanding of human interrelatedness and interdependence can contribute to their conversations. Again, he has planted a seed that can flower in the twenty-first century.

Protology, the Fallen Condition and Eschatology

Like other Christian theologians, Basil sees the human condition as undergoing fundamental transformations at different stages in salvation history. His reflection on what is most authentically human, like that of other Greek fathers, begins with his understanding of life in paradise before the Fall. It is noteworthy how many aspects of our present existence he regards as absent in that original condition, though he sees it not as a state of deprivation but as a state of plenitude filled with the glory of God. He presents Adam and Eve as lacking many things we know as good and instead enjoying greater things beyond our imagining. One wonders how many of the blessings we value in this life are actually poor substitutes for a fullness of life in God that can only be experienced here and now by saints and those like them.

Following Gen 1.29–30, he believes that in paradise people and animals were vegetarian; since none of them died, there was no meat for others to consume. He adds that God has allowed people to eat meat as a consolation for what they have lost through the Fall and their subsequent weakened condition. His attitude is to accept this concession with thanksgiving, yet he encourages those who seek zealously to return to the original state, that is, the ascetics, to be vegetarians. Subsequent Orthodox dietary practice follows the pattern he has prescribed, recommending that monastics abstain from meat but blessing others to eat it at appropriate times and seasons.

Moreover, Basil states, following Gen 2.25, that Adam and Eve needed no clothes for coverings in paradise and only needed them after the fall. Before that they gazed intently toward God and had no anxiety about their bodies. He adds that in time, if they had grown in holiness, God would have adorned them with robes of glory. Like Irenaeus and the Cappadocian Gregorys, he believes that God planned a process of spiritual maturation in paradise that was interrupted by human disobedience. He believes further that much of human culture as we know it has arisen as a way of managing the physical weakness and material scarcity that were not present in paradise. This begins with houses to provide shelter and includes agriculture, manufacturing, technology, commerce and the arts. Basil does not consider these things bad; rather, he acknowledges their necessity but considers them morally neutral and denies that they possess ultimate or permanent value. They belong to the present life, which will come to an end. The prospect of God's overwhelming judgment dwarfs their seeming importance when compared with the truly lasting goods, love for God and neighbor and practice of virtues and good works.

In the *Homily Explaining that God is Not the Cause of Evil*, Basil seeks to answer the puzzling question of how the first humans, who delighted in God's glory and every blessing in paradise, could ever have chosen to turn away from God. His response is essentially the same as that of the third-century theologian Origen, whose works he studied, though not uncritically. Basil states that Adam was so filled with the joys of God and the abundant life in the garden that he reached a state of satiety. This led to thoughtlessness and inattention, so that the gaze of his mind strayed from God and then became focused on material pleasures instead. Another major factor was the devil's deception. This raises a further question of how an angel could have fallen. Basil's answer is similar. Lucifer's catastrophic movement away from God began with a small lapse of attention. Basil compares it to the movement of an eye turning away from light into shadow.

For him Christians are always called to look toward the eschaton and order their priorities in light of it. He regards the life to come following the resurrection as at the very least[12] a restoration of the original paradisal state. He asks people to live as if this defines their true identity and purpose as human beings. This means taking to heart and acting in accordance with the values and priorities of the kingdom, as Christ presents them in the Gospels. Christians are thus called to a radical reorientation and transformation in their mode of existence. Basil taught this to his monastic communities, yet he really intended it for everyone and sought to reform the whole of society along these lines. He is a profound theologian and biblical interpreter, but his concerns are always practical, and he took the lead in living by what he believed and teaching others to do the same.

[12]Surely a greater communion with God will be present as well since God has united himself to humankind in the Incarnation. However, Basil does not address this point in the texts translated in this book, though perhaps he hints at it in *Long Rules*, Question 2.

On the Origin of Humanity, Discourse 1: On that which is according to the Image

1   I have come to make full payment of an old debt whose repayment I have postponed, not through a preference for unkindness but through bodily illness, a debt most necessary and obligatory for your hearing. For indeed it would have been unjust if having been taught about wild beasts and fishes, domestic animals and birds, heaven and things concerning heaven, about earth and things on earth, we were not illumined from the divinely inspired Scripture about our own origin. For just as our eyes see external things but do not see themselves except where they encounter something smooth and hard, then the image reflected as if by reflux makes them see things that are behind them; so also our mind does not see itself otherwise than by examining the Scriptures. For the light reflected there becomes the cause of vision for each of us. Since we are without understanding, we do not scrutinize our own structure; we are ignorant of what we are and why we are. For we are settled in the greatest indifference to ourselves, not possessing things within reach of our knowledge, a knowledge of the smallest aspects of what is in us.

2   Effort has been spent in much diligent study of the human body that belongs to all of us. If you study medicine, you will find how

many things it describes to us, how many hidden vessels it has discovered in our internal structure through anatomical dissection, tunnels in the invisible, a single confluence from the body, the channels of breath, the pipelines of blood, the drawing of breath, the dwelling of a hearth of heat by the heart, the continuous movement of breath around the heart. There are thousands of observations concerning these things with which not one of us is acquainted, for nobody has the leisure to take on this field of research, neither does each know himself as he is. For we are satisfied to know the sky rather than ourselves. Do not despise the wonder that is in you. For you are small in your own reckoning, but the Word will disclose that you are great. Because of this wise David, examining and seeing himself exactly, says, "Wonderful is your knowledge from me" [Ps 138.6], I have discovered in wonder knowledge concerning you.

Why "from me"?

"Wonderful is your knowledge from me," and the craftsmanship that is in me, understanding by what wisdom my body is structured. From this small work of construction, I understand the great Fashioner.

3   "Let us make the human being according to our image and likeness" [Gen 1.26]. Recently Scripture showed in passing and showed sufficiently what this word is and to whom this word is addressed. The church has proof concerning these things; it has faith more sure than proof. "Let us make the human being." Begin to understand yourself henceforth. This saying is not written concerning any other things that were fashioned. Light came to be, and there was a simple command; God said, "Let there be light" [Gen 1.3]. Heaven came to be without deliberation concerning heaven. The stars came to be, and there was no deliberation beforehand about the stars. Sea and boundless ocean—by a command they were brought into being. Fish of all kinds were ordered to come into being. Wild beasts and domestic animals, swimming and flying creatures—he spoke, and they came to be. Here, the human being does not yet exist, and there

is deliberation concerning the human. He did not say, as with the others, "Let there be a human being." Learn well your own dignity. He did not cast forth your origin by a commandment, but there was counsel in God to consider how to bring the dignified living creature into life. "Let us make." The wise one deliberates, the Craftsman ponders. So did he lose his skill, and did he deliberate in anxiety as he created in his masterpiece completion and perfection and exactitude? Or rather did he intend to show you that you are perfect before God?

4   You have learned that there are two persons, the one who speaks and the one to whom the speech is addressed. Why did he not say, "Make," but, "Let us make a human being"?

That you may know the sovereignty, that in acknowledging the Father you may not reject the Son; that you may learn that the Father created through the Son, and the Son created by the Father's will; that you may glorify the Father in the Son, and the Son in the Holy Spirit. Thus you have been made a common work, that you may be a worshiper of both together, not dividing the worship but uniting the Godhead. See a history in the form [of the Biblical passage] and theology in [its] meaning. "And God made the human—Let us make" [Gen 1.27,26]. And it did not say, "And they made," so that you would not receive an occasion for polytheism. For if the person is introduced as a multiplicity, people would have become heedless in heaping up for themselves a great crowd of gods. Yet it says, "Let us make," that you may recognize Father and Son and Holy Spirit.

It says, "God made the human being," that you may unite the Godhead and unite not the hypostases but the power, that you may have one glory not divided in the worship, not divided into polytheism. It does not say, "The gods made the human being," but, "God made." The hypostasis of the Father is proper to him, and that of the Son is proper to him, and that of the Holy Spirit is proper to him.

Then why are there not three gods?

Because the Godhead is one. For that Godhead which I see in the

Father, the same also is in the Son; and that which is in the Holy
Spirit, the same also is in the Son. Since there is one form in each of
them, the causation from the Father is also the same in the Son.
Because of this, our worship and praise are also one. The prelude to
our creation is true theology.

5   "Let us make the human being according to our image and likeness" [Gen 1.26]. We have been created according to the image of
God.

In what sense are we according to the image of God? Let us
purify ourselves of an ill-informed heart, an uneducated conception
about God. If we came into being according to the image of God,
they say, God is of the same shape as ourselves; there are eyes in God
and ears, a head, hands, a behind on which to sit—for it says in
Scripture that God sits [Cf. Ps 46.9]—feet with which to walk. So is
not God like this? Put away from your heart unseemly fantasies.
Expel from your reason things not in accord with the greatness of
God. God is without structure and simple. Do not imagine a shape
in regard to him. Do not diminish the Great One in a Jewish way. Do
not enclose God in bodily concepts, nor circumscribe him according to your own mind. He is incomprehensible in greatness. Consider what a great thing is, and add to the greatness more than you
have conceived, and to the more add more, and be persuaded that
your thought does not reach boundless things. Do not conceive a
shape; God is understood from his power, from the simplicity of his
nature, not greatness in size. He is everywhere and surpasses all; and
he is intangible, invisible, who indeed escapes your grasp. He is not
circumscribed by size, nor encompassed by a shape, nor measured
by power, nor enclosed by time, nor bounded by limits. Nothing is
with God as it is with us.

6   How then does Scripture say that we have come into being
according to the image of God? Let us learn the things concerning
God and understand those concerning ourselves, that we do not

have that which is according to the image in our bodily shape. For the shape of a body is corruptible. The incorruptible is not depicted in the corruptible, nor is the corruptible an image of the incorruptible. The human body is different in youth and in old age, different in health than in sickness, different in fear than in happiness, different in abundance than in need, different in peace than in war. It has a different color when awake and when asleep; in one case more red blossoms, as heat goes to the outside, in the other case the heat cools to the depth. Therefore also the bodies of those sleeping are yellowish.

How then can what is changing be like the unchanging? What always remains the same like what never has stood still? It escapes us like flowing streams; before being seen it runs away. The human body appears one way, then another.

"In our image." Is something flowing the image of the immovable nature? The shaped of that which has no shape? How then shall we search out that which is according to the image? In the things which the Lord himself has said. If I say something of my own, do not receive it; if it is the Lord's, receive it indeed.

"Let us make the human being according to our image and likeness. And let them rule the fish" [Gen 1.26]. By the body or the mind? Is the ruling power in the soul or in the flesh? The flesh is weaker than that of many animals. What comparison is there between the flesh of the human being and the camel, the human and the ox, the human and any wild beast you like? The human flesh is easily captured and is attacked by the flesh of a wild beast.

But in what is the ruling principle?

In the superiority of reason. What is lacking in strength of body is encompassed by the employment of reason. How does the human being move great weights? By thought or bodily vigor?

7   "Let us make the human being according to our image." It speaks of the inner human being. "Let us make the human being." But you will ask, "Why does it not speak to us of the rational part?"

It says that the human being is according to the image of God, but the rational part is the human being. Listen to the apostle say, "Although our outer human being is perishing, the inner is renewed day by day" [2 Cor 4.16].

How?

I recognize two human beings, one the sense-perceptible, and one hidden under the sense-perceptible, invisible, the inner human. Therefore we have an inner human being, and we are somehow double, and it is truly said that we are that which is within. For I am what concerns the inner human being, the outer things are not me but mine. For I am not the hand, but I am the rational part of the soul. And the hand is a limb of the human being. Therefore the body is an instrument of the human being, an instrument of the soul, and the human being is principally the soul in itself.

"Let us make the human being according to our image," that is, let us give him the superiority of reason.

8   "And let them rule." Not, "Let us make the human being, and let them be angry and lustful and sorrowful," for the passions are not included in the image of God, but the reason is master of the passions. "And let them rule the fish." As soon as you are made, you are also made ruler. "And let them rule." When receiving authority for one year from the emperor, as a human from a human, as a mortal from a mortal, one receives it from one who does not truly possess it, for what authority does a human being receive in the soul? But you received it from God, not written on wooden tablets, nor on perishable leaves wasted on moths, but your nature has the divine voice inscribed in it, "Let them rule." All these things belong to the human realm. "Let them rule the fish, the wild animals of the earth, the creatures that fly in the air, the domestic animals, the reptiles that creep on the earth" [Gen 1.26]. It does not say, "Let us make the human being according to our image and likeness, and let them eat of every fruit tree which has fruit in itself." The things of the flesh are second, the priorities of the soul are first.

First the power to rule was conferred on you. O human, you are a ruling being. And why do you serve the passions as a slave? Why do you throw away your own dignity and become a slave of sin? For what reason do you make yourself a prisoner of the devil? You were appointed ruler of creation, and you have renounced the nobility of your own nature.

Suppose "you were called as a slave" [1 Cor 7.21]. Why do you lament your slavery in the body? Why do you not consider great the sovereignty given you by God, that you have reason as master of the passions? When you see your master being a slave to pleasure, while you yourself are a slave only in body, know that you are a slave in name only. He has the name of master, but he has established his slavery by deed. You see him joining with a prostitute, but you despise her. How are you not master of your passion, while your master is slave of the pleasures you have trodden beneath yourself?

Therefore, "Let us make the human being, and let him rule;" where the power to rule is, there is the image of God.

9   "Let them rule the fish." The rule was first given to us over those living far away. It did not say, "Let them rule the domestic animals," but, "the fish." For their life is in the water. Therefore the rule of the fish was given to us first.

And how do we rule the fish?

Do you know how creatures appear beside you in a tidal pool, how your shadow scares all of them away? What master of a house thus produces calm when a clamor of household crowds arises, and makes all things share in good order through the presence of the ruler? How does the whole aquatic creation, at the appearance of one human being, change form? It no longer has freedom of movement in its way of life; it does not boldly swim up to the surface of the sea or the tidal pool.

Whenever the dolphin observes that a human being is nearby, although the dolphin is the most royal of the aquatic beasts, it stands in awe. Thus the rule over the swimming creatures was given to the human. And whenever you see your own reason penetrating all things and governing all things, how do you not rule the aquatic beasts?

I myself saw the ingenuity of human beings. They made a device of certain fishhooks and attached to them baits proportionate to the size of the aquatic beast swallowing them; then at the top of the cords from which the fishhooks are hung, extending a bag of air and hanging them from the top, they release it on the surface of the sea. Therefore as the wild aquatic beast is drawn to the baits and receives into itself the fishhooks, it drags the float toward the bottom. But the nature of the float carries it upward, so it pulls again toward the surface. And having been pierced by their own food, roaming eagerly up and down, the aquatic beasts search the deep, they again traverse the sea of seas, and their great labor is ineffectual; at last with that fishhook they become easy to capture. Tamed by labor, subdued by hunger, dragged dead by the floats, the beast becomes prey to the hunter. The great belongs to the small, the huge to the weak.

Why?

Because receiving the power to rule through the superiority of reason, the human being leads the most disobedient toward order like runaway slaves; those whom he is unable to draw to himself through great gentleness are of necessity enslaved. Thus everywhere the power to rule given by the Creator is innate in the human. Therefore swordfish and hammer-headed sharks and whales and sawfish and cowfish and all those called fearful among aquatic beasts have come to be subject to humans.

10 "Let them rule the fish of the sea and the wild beasts of the earth." Have you not seen the mighty, roaring lion, of whom even the name is intolerable, and whose roar makes the earth tremble? For who can endure to withstand his attack? None of the animals trusts enough in its own superiority of power to stand against the attack of a lion. But all the same you see the lion shut in a small cage. Who has confined him? Who has contrived the small prison for the big

animal? Who, while providing through the narrowness of the wooden bars for the beast's respiration, so as not to suffocate him by his own breathing, yet gives him free respiration while controlling security? Who? Is it not the human being? He makes the fiercest of beasts into playthings.

Does he not mock at the leopards, when he stretches out a piece of paper fashioned into a human shape? And the beast tears apart the paper, while the human being lying beneath it laughs at the beast's folly. Does not the human rule all things by his superiority?

What do I say to you concerning the flying creatures? The human being does not ascend into the air, but he flies along with the winged creatures by the power of thought. For nothing holds back thought. It searches through things in the deep, it pursues things on the earth, it grasps beforehand things in the air.

Have you observed when a bird sitting on a top branch laughs at human beings? For it has trusted in the great lightness of its wing. But still one can see a child at play placing reeds beneath reeds and on top of the reeds attaching glue, then deceptively hiding the presence of the glue among the branches and the foliage, and lifting his eye upward. By a small touch he has ruled the bird. The one traversing the air, the winged creature borne through the ether, he has led captive by the glue. The human being remains below, his hand below, but his mind ascends, and through skill all things become accessible to the human. He sets traps for the winged creatures, archers aim at those who fly, with baits he hunts the hungry beasts.

Have you not also observed an eagle falling violently upon prey, then being caught by the trap below? Thus the highest creature comes down, dragged by human baits. God has placed all things in submission to the hand of the human being. He has completed the creation and has not left the human without a share in domination. Do not say, "How the creatures borne in the air surpass me!" Through reason they also come to be in submission to you.

"And of the reptiles that creep on the earth." Do you see in what sense you have come into being according to the image of God?

11   "And God made the human being." What then is the human being?

Relying on those we have read and those we have heard, we will define him. For there is no longer a need for us to borrow foreign definitions, nor to introduce the ideas of vanity into the reasoning of the truth. The human is a rational creature of God, having come into being according to the image of his Creator. If something is lacking to this concept, let those who have spent much in acquiring the perishable wisdom examine it. According to the image of God the human came into being.

12   "And God blessed the human being, and said, Grow and multiply and fill the earth" [Gen 1.28]. This blessing was also given to the fishes. "And God said, 'Let the waters bring forth reptiles with living souls,' and thus it came to be" [Gen 1.20]. "And again God said, 'Grow and multiply and fill the waters' " [Gen 1.22].

What then surpasses this?

These words necessarily concern both the things given you in common with other creatures and the things reserved as proper to you. For you grow as do the rest of the living creatures. From a little thing at first by small additions you come to maturity. Thus also do horses and dogs, thus also eagles and swans, and all those of which you might speak. From their initial littleness at conception by small additions they attain the maturity of growth. Then through decline they again return to a lesser stature. Therefore the things that were common to nature were also given to you.

13   "Grow," that is, grow up. You are born small; become big, and let there be a limit to your growth. If we grow in the first seven years and we advance in stature in the second period of seven years, we are not similarly obliged in every part of our life to grow in each seven-year period.

The first seven-year period contains the age of childhood. The limits of the age of childhood are manifest in the replacement of teeth. Some have fallen out, others have grown from beneath them. Growth makes a second beginning, leading to the completion of the fourteenth year. It is the second segment of childhood; first comes the small child, then the child. Then comes the youth, then the man, from the fourteenth year; herein are the limits of growth. Therefore, "grow." If you reach a hundred years, you do not admit of growth from the first to the hundredth year, but this one word "grow," spoken wisely, structures things providentially.

"Grow," to what point?

But there is no measure of growth. With the first structure brought into being in the womb, the principles of growth were also brought into being. For the gift that afterward comes into being with age is not new, but the things brought into being within the mother also receive at that time the characteristics most useful for growth. The teeth fall out, and we know there has been growth to a certain measure. The father measures the child of three years; he knows that it will receive twice this size at the completion of this period. For the child will grow to twice the stature it has at three years, and then to twice this stature again when grown. For this is the measure of human nature, as far as there is a boundary, as far as there is a limit, from the first seven-year period to the second. After that the heat becomes greater, the body's excellence is molded, the moisture is left behind, the limbs are strengthened, human beings are at the beginning of the stronger part of youth, without yet possessing maturity. For their flesh is still newly made, and it is unsuited for the endurance of labors. At this point the living being has received lightness and agility. In the third seven-year period, he then receives the completion of youth. And there is still an increase in the height of the body.

After the third seven year period, whenever the body recovers from the work of growing in height, it begins to move to broadening, and as it were to establish a firm foundation all around for what has been raised up, and to place thickness around it, and to strengthen the limbs of the body. Nature makes these things according to its own sequential order. It came into being from the beginning by the Lord's command, and what was spoken then traverses the whole creation as far as the end.

14   "Grow and multiply." "Grow," that the creation may not be delimited within one condition. "Multiply," that it may not exist only in one person, but rather in many. "And fill the earth;" but do not fill it by settling it all, for then we would have lived crowded together, if the earth corresponded in size to our habitations; but fill it by authority, which God has given us to dominate the earth.

"Fill the earth." Not of course the burned and uncultivated and frozen and inaccessible regions; humans are not of course required to fill such places. God has made us masters so as to fill it, and we fill the earth by our reason. When we see the extent of burned and uninhabited earth, when we see what the northern region is, which because of excessive cold is uncultivated and unusable, have we not filled the earth? After having chosen what is useful, have we not rejected what is useless for human life? Thus, the command to "fill the earth" has made us masters. It is not because we do not use all of it that we do not dominate all of it. For when you buy wheat, are you not master of all of it, although you have in the wheat some that is edible and some that is thrown away? Do you not throw away the stones as useless and anything else mixed with the food that is unusable, blow away the chaff and separate out the darnel, and choose the pure wheat for the maintenance of life? It is similar with the earth. One part, the best, has received what is useful for habitation, another part is necessary for cultivation, the rest is left for the grazing of quadrupeds.

Say to me, "Will not what I choose be arranged, since I have become master according to the gift of the Lord who created me?"

"And multiply. Let them rule the fish of the sea, the flying creatures of the sky, and the wild beasts of the earth." This is the blessing, this is the legislation, this is the honor given us by God.

15 "And God made the human being. According to the image of God he made him" [Gen 1.27]. So then, did you not say that the proposition was incomplete? "Let us make the human being according to our image and likeness." The plan had two parts, "according to the image" and "according to the likeness." The creative work was one. Could he have planned it one way and re-planned something else? Could some regret have followed regarding the creation? Was there a debility in the Creator, who chose one thing and made another? Or is there idle talk in the words? Or perhaps it is saying the same thing. "Let us make the human according to our image and likeness." Yet to say "according to the image" is not to say "according to the likeness." Whichever we choose, we would be rejecting what has been written. For if it says the same, it is perverse to say the same things twice. To say there is an idle word in Scripture is a terrible blasphemy. But indeed it does not speak idly. Therefore it is necessary that the human come into being according to the image and according to the likeness.

Why has it not been said, "And God made the human being according to the image of God and according to the likeness"? Was the Creator exhausted?

The idea is impious!

Did the one giving the order change his purpose?

The thought is even more impious!

But did he speak and change his plan?

No, neither does Scripture say this, nor is the Creator exhausted, nor was the counsel frustrated. What is the meaning of the text's silence?

16 "Let us make the human being according to our image and according to our likeness" [Gen 1.26]. By our creation we have the first, and by our free choice we build the second. In our initial structure co-originates and exists our coming into being according to the image of God. By free choice we are conformed to that which is according to the likeness of God. And this is what is according to free

choice: the power exists in us but we bring it about by our activity. If the Lord, in anticipation, had not said in making us, "Let us make," and, "according to our likeness," if he had not given us the power to come to be according to the likeness, we would not have received the likeness to God by our own authority. Yet now he has made us with the power to become like God. And in giving us the power to become like God, he let us be artisans of the likeness to God, so that the reward for the work would be ours. Thus we would not be like images made by a painter, lying inertly, lest our likeness should bring praise to another. For when you see an image exactly shaped like the prototype, you do not praise the image, but you marvel at the painter. Accordingly, so that the marvel may become mine and not another's, he has left it to me to become according to the likeness of God. For I have that which is according to the image in being a rational being, but I become according to the likeness in becoming Christian.

17   "Become perfect as your heavenly Father is perfect" [Mt 5.48]. Do you see how the Lord restores to us that which is according to the likeness? "For he makes his sun rise upon evil and good, and he sends rain upon just and unjust" [Mt 5.45]. If you become a hater of evil, free of rancor, not remembering yesterday's enmity; if you become brother-loving and compassionate, you are like God. If you forgive your enemy from your heart, you are like God. If as God is toward you, the sinner, you become the same toward the brother who has wronged you, by your good will from your heart toward your neighbor, you are like God. As you have that which is according to the image through your being rational, you come to be according to the likeness by undertaking kindness. Take on yourself "a heart of compassion, kindness," that you may put on Christ. For through those things by which you undertake sympathy you put on Christ, and drawing near to him is drawing near to God. Thus the creation story is an education in human life. "Let us make the human being in our image." Let him have by his creation that which is according to the

image, let him also come to be according to the likeness. For this God gave the power. If he created you also according to the likeness, what would be yours to give? Through what would you be crowned? For if the Fashioner gave you the whole of it, how would the kingdom of heaven be opened to you? But now the one is given, the other is left incomplete; that you may complete yourself, become worthy of the recompense by God.

Then how do we come to be according to the likeness?

Through the Gospels.

What is Christianity?

Likeness to God as far as is possible for human nature. If you are shown to be a Christian, hasten to become like God, put on Christ. But how will you put him on if you have not been sealed? How will you put him on while not receiving baptism? While not receiving the garment of incorruption? If you reject the likeness to God? If I said to you, "Become like a king," would you not consider me a benefactor? When I wish to make you like God, do you flee the word which divinizes you, stopping your ears, that you may not hear the saving words?

18   "And God made the human being according to his image." "The [masc.] human being," says the woman, "What does that have to do with me? The man came to be, for it does not say the [fem.] human being," she says, "but by setting forth the [masc.] human being, it implies the masculine."[1] But that nobody may ignorantly ascribe the name of human only to the man, it adds, "Male and female he created them" [Gen 1.27]. The woman also possesses creation according to the image of God, as indeed does the man. The natures are alike of equal honor, the virtues are equal, the struggles equal, the judgment alike. Let her not say, "I am weak." The weakness is in the flesh, in the soul is the power. Since indeed that which is according to God's image is of equal honor, let the virtue be of equal honor, the

[1]See Introduction.

showing forth of good works. There is no excuse for one who wishes to allege that the body is weak. And why is it simply delicate? But through compassion it is vigorous in patient endurance and earnest in vigils. When has the nature of man been able to match the nature of woman in patiently passing through her own life? When has man been able to imitate the vigor of women in fastings, the love of toil in prayers, the abundance in tears, the readiness for good works?

I have seen a woman secretly committing good thefts, doing good works apart from her husband for the sake of her husband, for the sake of the household's growth, for the sake of the children's long life. She gives and hides it from her husband's knowledge, distributing alms for his sake and concealing it from him. For since the Creator sees the things that are hidden, she does not make public her well-doing.

The good woman has that which is according to the image. Do not cling to the outer human being, it is molded [like clay]. The soul is placed within, under the coverings and the delicate body. Soul indeed is equal in honor to soul; in the coverings is the difference.

Therefore you have become like God through kindness, through endurance of evil, through communion, through love for one another and love for the brethren, being a hater of evil, dominating the passions of sin, that to you may belong the rule.

19   "And let them rule the fish." It was given to you to rule the irrational fish, thus you became ruler of irrational passion.

"And let them rule the wild beasts." You rule every wild beast. So, you say, what beasts do I have in myself? Indeed you have thousands, and a great crowd of beasts in yourself. And do not consider this statement to be an outrage. Anger is a little beast when it barks in the heart. Is it not wilder than every dog? Is not the deceit lurking in a deceitful soul harder to tame than every lurking bear? Is not hypocrisy a beast? Is not one sharp in insults a scorpion? Is not one who in hiding strikes out in revenge more dangerous than a viper? Is the greedy person not a rapacious wolf? What kind of beast is not in us? Is not the one mad for women a raging horse? For Scripture says, "They have become horses mad for women, each neighing toward his neighbor's wife" [Jer 5.8]. It does not say he spoke to the woman, but he neighed. It transferred him to the nature of those without reason, because of the passion with which he associated himself. Therefore there are many beasts in us.

Have you truly become ruler of beasts if you rule those outside but leave those within ungoverned? Will you rule truly in ruling the lion by your reason and despising its roar, but gnashing your teeth and emitting inarticulate sounds as the anger within all at once strives to attack? What is more dangerous than this, when a human being is ruled by passion, when anger pushes reason aside, not consenting to remain within, and takes upon itself governance of the soul?

You are indeed created ruler, ruler of passions, ruler of beasts, ruler of creeping things, ruler of winged creatures. Do not have airy thoughts, nor be light and unstable in mind. You were appointed to rule winged things. You are out of place if you strike down external flying things, yourself being light and lofty. Do not be filled with smoke, do not be flighty, do not think things greater than human nature; when complimented, do not go above nature, do not glorify yourself, do not consider yourself to be something great. For thus you will be an unstable winged creature, carried about this way and that by an unsteady nature.

Rule the thoughts in yourself, that you may become ruler of all beings. Thus the rule we have been given over the animals trains us to rule the things belonging to ourselves. For it is misplaced to be governed at home and govern nations, to be ruled within by a prostitute and be mayor of the city by public consent. It is necessary that household affairs be managed well and that good order within be arranged, and thus to receive authority over others. Since the word of Scripture will be turned back at you by those you rule if your household affairs are disorderly and disorganized, namely "Physician, heal yourself" [Lk 4.23]. let us heal ourselves first.

Nobody is condemned for not catching a lion, but one who will not govern anger is ridiculous to everyone. So one who does not prevail over his own passion is led to condemnation, while one who cannot prevail over wild beasts does not appear to have done anything worthy of blame.

20 May the Lord who has provided what is written, who has also enabled our small and weak tongue to converse thus with you, who through our weak reason has intimated a great treasure for you in the few outlines of truth, give to you through small things great things, through a few seeds the perfection of knowledge; may he grant to us the complete reward of our free choice and that you be fulfilled in the fruit of your enjoyment of divine words, and thereby to him be glory and dominion unto ages of ages. Amen.

On the Origin of Humanity, Discourse 2: On the human being

1   The wise Solomon, made wise "not in a wisdom of persuasive words" [1 Cor 2.4], but in teachings of the Holy Spirit, glorified the human being in what we have just read. He cried out, saying, "The human being is great, and a merciful man is honored" [Prov 20.6]. But as for me, I searched vainly concerning myself through what I had in my mind and read in Scripture regarding the human. For I reasoned in this way: how is the human great, that perishable living being subjected to a thousand passions, enduring a swarm of innumerable evils from birth to old age, concerning whom it has been said, "Lord, what is the human being, that you are made known to him?" [Ps 143.3] The Psalmist despises the living being as worthless, but the Proverb glorifies the human as something great.

2   But for me the history of the human being's creation that has been read resolves this kind of question. For now we heard that God took "dust from the earth" and "molded the human being" [Gen 2.7]. I discovered from this word both that the human is nothing and that the human is great. If you look toward our nature alone, it is nothing and is worthy of nothing, but if you look toward the honor with which he was honored, the human is great.

What is that?

"God said, let there be light, and light came to be" [Gen 1.3]. Compare the creation of the human and the creation of light. There it says, "Let a firmament come to be" [Gen 1.6]. The great heaven, having been stretched out above us, came to be by a word of God. Stars and sun and moon, and all things which we contemplate with the eye and which we behold above as great, have being by a word. Sea and land and what is set in order in them, all kinds of species of animals, diverse varieties of plants, all these have come to be by a word.

But what about the human being?

It was not said, "Let a human come to be," as, "Let a firmament come to be," but you see something more in the human. Above light, above heaven, above luminaries, above all things is the creation of the human being. "The Lord God took." Our body is quite worthy to be entirely molded by his own hands. He did not command an angel. The earth did not automatically cast us forth as it did the cicadas. He did not tell the ministering angelic powers to make this or that. But by his own hands, as an artist, he took earth. When you focus on what is taken, what is the human being? When you understand the One doing the molding, the human is great, indeed he is nothing because of the material and great through the honor.

3   "And God took." But how is it that one finds in the preceding words, "And God made the human being" [Gen 1.27], but here Scripture speaks anew of human creation. As if we had learned nothing about the human, the story says, "And God took dust from the earth, and God molded the human being" [Gen 2.7]. Already some have said that "molded" is said of the body while "made" is said of the soul. Probably the idea is not outside the truth. For as it says, "And God made the human being, according to the image of God he created him" [Gen 1.27], it says "made;" but as the narrative passes to our bodily existence, it says "molded." The Psalmist teaches the difference between making and molding when he says, "Your hands made me and molded me" [Ps 118.73]. He made the inner human being, he molded the outer. For indeed molding is suited to dust, making to that which is according to the image. As the flesh was molded, the soul was made.

4   So then having spoken about the subsistence of the soul, now Scripture discusses the molding of the body. Keep this argument in mind. What is my other point? That the one is said "in the beginning," while the other is handed down concerning the manner in which we have come into being. First it said that God indeed created; in what follows it also says how he created. For if it simply said that he created, you would have thought that he created us in the same way as the domestic animals, as the wild beasts, as the plants, as the grass. Therefore so that you may flee fellowship with the wild creatures, the Word has transmitted the particular loving skill of God concerning you. "God took dust from the earth" [Gen 2.7]. There it says that he created, here how he created. He took dust from the earth and molded it with his own hands.

Ponder how you were molded. Consider the workshop of nature. The hand that received you is God's. May what is molded by God not be defiled by evil, not be altered by sin; may you not fall from the hand of God. You are a vessel divinely molded, having come into being from God. Glorify your Creator. For you came to be for the sake of no other thing except that you be an instrument fit for the glory of God. And for you this whole world is as it were a book that proclaims the glory of God, announcing through itself the hidden and invisible greatness of God to you who have a mind for the apprehension of truth. So be mindful of all the things that have been said.

5   "And God blessed them and said, Grow and multiply, and fill the earth" [Gen 1.28]. Growth is of two kinds, that of the body and that of the soul. But growth of the soul is progress to perfection through things learned, while bodily growth is development from smallness to the appropriate stature.

Thus "grow" is said to the irrational animals in regard to perfection of body, in regard to the completion of nature; but to us "grow" is said according to the inner human being, according to the progress which is growth into God. Such was Paul, stretching out to the things before, forgetting the things behind [cf. Phil 3.13]. This is growth in visions, acquisition of piety, extending toward the better, as we ever reach toward truly existing things, ever leaving the things that came before to seek what is lacking to piety, as far as this is required. Such was Isaac, concerning whom this testimony has been written: "Advancing, he raised himself up while he became great" [Gen 26.13]. For he did not turn away, nor did he remain small in growth, but he ever advanced, crossing to great things. He passed over to the works of virtue, he crossed through self-control with a great stride, he arrived at justice, from there he ascended to courage, Thus the just one climbs to the summit of the height of good. The "growth," therefore, is a growth according to God, a perfection according to the inner human being.

"Multiply." This blessing pertains to the church. Let the theology not be circumscribed in one person, but let the Gospel of salvation be proclaimed to all the earth.

"Multiply." Who?

Those engendered according to the Gospel.

"Fill the earth." Fill the flesh which has been given you for serving through good works. Let the eye be filled with seeing duties. Let the hand be filled with good works. May the feet stand ready to visit the sick, journeying to fitting things. Let every usage of our limbs be filled with actions according to the commandments. This is to "fill the earth."

Thus these words are common also to the irrational animals, but they have a specific meaning when we apply them to that which is according to the image and that with which we have been honored. For they grow bodily, but we grow spiritually; and they fill the earth with multitudes, but we fill the earth connected to us with good actions, that is, bodily service.

6   "Behold, I have given you every tree which has fruit in itself; it will be to you for food" [Gen 1.29]. Let the church not skip over anything. All things are prescriptive. It does not say, "I have given you

the fishes for food, I have given you the domestic animals, the reptiles, the quadrupeds." For he did not create these things for this purpose, as Scripture says. But the first legislation granted enjoyment of fruits, for we were still reckoned to be worthy of paradise.

And what is the mystery present for you in what is hidden here?

To you, the wild beasts and the birds the fruits are given, it says, and the green plants and the grass. "For you as food, to the birds of the sky and all the wild beasts of the earth" [Cf. Gen 1.30]. Yet indeed we see many of the wild beasts do not eat fruit. With what fruit does the leopard accept to be nourished? And what fruit can feed a lion?

But these animals in the same way, subjected to the law of nature, were sustained by fruits. But when the human being changed his habits and went outside the limit given him, after the flood, the Lord, knowing the humans to be profligate, granted them the enjoyment of all foods. "Eat all these things as you do green vegetables" [Gen 9.3]. By this concession the rest of living beings also received the freedom to eat them.

For this cause the lion is a carnivore, for this cause also vultures await carcasses. For doubtless indeed vultures did not look around the earth when living things came to birth. For nothing died of these things given meaning or brought into existence by God, so that vultures might eat it. Nature was not divided, for it was in its prime; nor did hunters kill, for that was not yet the custom of human beings; nor did wild beasts claw prey, for they were not carnivores. And it is customary for vultures to feed on corpses, but since there were not yet corpses, not yet their stench, so there was not yet such food for vultures. But all followed the diet of swans and all grazed the meadows. And as we often see dogs grazing on grass for the sake of healing, not since it is the food natural to them, but since the nonrational animals by some teaching of nature come untaught upon what is useful, we also consider the carnivorous animals then [in paradise] to be such, to regard grass as their food, not plotting against each other.

7   But the restoration after the present age will be such as was the first creation. And the human being will come again to his original condition, rejecting evil, this life of many troubles, the soul's enslavement involving life's concerns; putting aside all these things, he will return to that life in paradise unenslaved to the passions of the flesh, free, intimate with God, with the same way of life as the angels.

Therefore we have said these things, not that we wish to exclude the use of foods given us by God, but that we may bless the past time. As life was, it was without want of more. How little human beings needed to lead their life; the cause of our variety in diet was the introduction of sin. For since we fell away from the true delight that was in paradise, we invented adulterated delicacies for ourselves. And since we no longer see the tree of life, nor do we pride ourselves in that beauty, there have been given to us for our enjoyment cooks and bakers, and various pastries and aromas, and such things console us in our banishment from there.

As indeed the sick, when struck down by a violent illness, cannot participate in their accustomed enjoyments, they receive perfumes and the like from their doctors as greetings. For since they have lost the enjoyment of stronger people, those who flatter their senses contrive means adapted to their weakness. However, now indeed as we wish to conduct ourselves in imitation of the life of paradise, we avoid this excessively material enjoyment of foods, conducting ourselves as far as is possible according to that life, using fruits and grains and the produce of fruit trees for passing through life, but what surpasses these things we reject as unnecessary. For though the rest is not abominable to the Creator, neither is it chosen for the enjoyment of the flesh.

8   "And God rested from all his works the seventh day" [Gen 2.2]. As for the mathematicians and those who have studied such things and have proposed knowledge regarding this as something great, let them say that the number six is akin to the creation of the world,

since it is fruitful, generating many figures of numbers from itself, and perfect in its own parts; and of those matters regarding six-ness which mathematicians pursue in their scholarly discussions, let one speak elsewhere if there is leisure. Let them also say regarding seven-ness that there is something sterile in the number seven; for nothing is born from it, nor is the number seven born from another. And that I may not lead the discourse into this abundant material, sidetracking my discussion with you, I will go on to more sensible things.

But if someone has experience of these things, let him know that we also hold in store the treasure of these things. So if arithmetic is great, the seeds of arithmetic are here. But we, considering these things to be from the wisdom of the world, do not here take pride in stealing small things from what to them is great. Now, that we may show them that the things they seek after eagerly are to us contemptible, we pass by discussion of these matters in silence. Furthermore, the theory concerning these things is not easily grasped by all the people. And the church assembled here does not expect a lecture on paradoxical concepts but seeks the resolution of problems with a view to edification.

9   The seventh day has been honored as the Sabbath. The number seven is honored by the Jews, which determines the feasts of Tabernacles and Trumpets and the Day of Atonement [cf. Lev 23.24–36; Num 29.1]. They honor the seventh year, which is called the time of release [cf. Deut 15.1–3]. For they had six years to work the land, but in the seventh year what grew by itself sufficed when they possessed the land of promise [cf. Lev 25.2–5]. The Hebrew was a slave for six years and in the seventh was released from slavery [cf. Ex 21.2]. In the seventieth year captivity was loosed by them [cf. Jer 25.11–12, 29.10]. But we also find things pertaining to us. "Seven times," Scripture says, "the just man falls and rises again" [Prov 24.16]. In this way we approach seven-ness. Enoch, seventh from the creation, did not see death [cf. Gen 5.24]; this is a mystery of the church. Moses, seventh from Abraham, received the law, which is the transformation of life,

the deliverance from lawlessness, the introduction of justice, the presence of God, good order in the world, the legislation of things to be done. In the seventy-seventh generation from Adam, Christ appeared [cf. Lk 3.23–38].

10   Peter knows the mystery of seven-ness. "How many times, if my brother sins against me, should I forgive him? As many as seven times?" [Mt 18.21–22]. He knows little of the mystery. He has not yet learned, for he is still a disciple. "As many as seven times?" The Teacher does not reject the seven; the disciple speaks of what he has known. The Master surpasses the wealth; "How many times does he sin and I forgive?"

Why does Peter not say, "as many as six times," "as many as eight times," but, "as many as seven times"? Why does the Lord not say, "as many as a hundred times a hundred times," but multiplies the number seven?

Neither did Peter ask for a different way, nor did the Lord depart from the rule of seven-ness. Peter observed that the rule is an ancient tradition, seven-ness bears a certain image of remission of sins, that is the complete rest of which the Sabbath is a sign, the seventh day after the creation. Peter reaches seven times, the Lord as far as seventy times seven.

Sins are avenged seven times. Is it not written, "Anyone who kills Cain will be done away, since he is avenged seven times" [Gen 4.15]? Not eight times but seven.

For what reason?

Wait a little, and you will discover the mystery. The first sin is avenged seven times; the second is the murder of Lamech: "So if Cain was avenged seven times, Lamech will be avenged seventy times seven" [Gen 4.24]. And if there is a seventh forgiveness by Peter, referring to the vengeance of Cain, there is consent by the Lord to seventy times seven, as the condemnation for Lamech is seventy times seven. As great as the transgression is, so great also is the gift of grace. Where there is little sin, there also is little forgiveness, for one to whom little is forgiven also loves little [cf. Lk 7.47]. "Where sin abounded, grace superabounded" [Rom 5.20].

What then is the mystery?

The eighth day is said to be the age of judgment, in which the sinner will be punished seven times, the extreme sinner seventy times seven times. The just person will be honored seven times, the extremely just seventy times seven times. Now the kindness of God shows us through enigmas a glimpse of the things to come, but at the time of the second coming the truth is manifest and clear; it will show who is worthy of what recompense. Accordingly, the Lord grants sevenfold to us sinners the remission of our debts, if here we propitiate him through confession and repentance. So, since we know that fearful day, and since the remission of sins has been granted, as through repentance we offer a worthy compensation commensurate with the faults we have committed, may we do away with our sins, so that there we may escape the toilsome multiplication of the debt. We would call this the seventh day in relation to the consummation of the eighth day in that age.

11   "And God rested from his works" [Gen 2.2]. There will be no more works of this world in that day, no more marriages, no more business dealings, no more agriculture. But the whole earth will be terrified, all the creation in turmoil, the sweat inconsolable, even the just in turmoil regarding what lot then will be disclosed for them. Even Abraham will be in turmoil then, not lest he be condemned to Gehenna, but wondering in which rank of the just he will be placed, first or second or third. The Lord comes from the heavens, and the heavens are shattered, power reveals itself, the whole creation is trembling. Who is without fear? Not even the angels. They are also present, though not to give an account to God, but the glorious epiphany likewise hurls them all into trembling. Do you not hear what Isaiah is saying: "If you open the heaven, the mountains will be seized with trembling because of you" [Is 64.1]. Thus the sea becomes solid, thus the creation ceases, nature is made dead. All

striving through words achieves nothing in the face of the visitation from the heavens. Then the just are snatched away, then the clouds are the vehicle of the just, then the angels are escorts of the just, then the just as stars are lifted up from earth into heaven; but the sinners are bound, fettered by the burden of their own sins, they will fall downward with bad consciences.

Accordingly, that seven is prefigured by this seven. "And God rested from all his works." The things of this life will no longer be in that day. The desires of youth have been stilled, there is no more proposal of marriage; no more desire for procreation; regarding gold, no concern. You, the avaricious, have forgotten your purse; you, the property owner, have forgotten the land; you, mad for fame, have forgotten the glory. All those things have flown from the mind. And the soul stands before the Fearful One, before the expectation of impending terrors. For fear banishes every passionate thought that has gained citizenship in our souls. Where there is fear of God, all the stains of passion are driven out of our thoughts. This seventh day is truly a type of that seventh day.

12   "And God took dust from the earth, and God molded the human being" [Gen 2.7]. The creation of the world was not finished; the sequence was not interrupted to bypass the narrative concerning us, but it said, "God made the human, and he rested from all his works." And after he rested, Scripture teaches us how he created. "God took dust from the earth."

When you hear of dust, learn not to fear. Do not judge a human being by his appearance. What do you consider great in yourself? Where thoughts come to you that bring swelling and inflammation in the heart, let the memory of the creation enter into you, how you were created. "God took dust from the earth, and God molded the human being." When can you forget what is your own? You forget what is your own when you withdraw from the earth. If you never depart from the earth but remain connatural with the earth, walk on the earth, rest on the earth, give judgment on the earth—for indeed everything, whether great or small, that you do is on the earth—you have nearby the memory of your lowliness.

Are you violent and hot-tempered? From where does anger come to you? From disgrace? You cannot listen to the disclosure of your lowly birth? Immediately anger boils over in you? You compete to say something worse than what you have heard? Lower your glance, and let anger cease for you. See the earth and take it to heart. He said I am lowly born, who have been born from the earth. He said less than what I am, for he did not say I am from the earth, but from a human being; but how much more honorable is a human endowed with soul than the earth that is walked on? And I see the ancient earth as my mother, so it is not an outrage to be born from a slave, but an honor to be born endowed with soul. The one who thought to outrage me was unaware that the one outraged was honored more. For I, having understanding of my own nature, know who I am and from whence I came.

Thus the remembrance that we have come from earth never allows anger to awaken. Let the earth, always present and remembered, be an ally to reason.

13   When you hasten in desire, it is through the earth that you run; take to heart how you originated. If you take to heart that you will be dissolved into earth, the madness of desire ceases. "You are earth and to earth you will return" [Gen 3.19]. Remember that in a little while these limbs which now throb, or the present desire of the flesh, will not be, as the limbs are decomposed and dissolved into earth. Remember nature, and let every impulse toward evil cease. Let this remembrance be for us a safeguard against all sin.

"God molded the human being of dust from the earth." Humility is good, this memory conformed to nature. If it said, "God molded the human being, taking something heavenly," when would we see this thing, that we might remember our nature? From things nearby the remembrance of our nothingness is present to us, from that on which we walk. Nod toward the earth, and understand that from what is akin to the earth, from things discarded by you, you were shaped. What is more contemptible than ourselves? What is more fit to set at nought than ourselves?

Have you seen someone conceited, clothed in bright colored raiment, his hand bearing a ring, its setting holding a precious stone, and he is conceited about this? He wears cloth of silk, possesses household servants with long golden hair, and struts too elaborately, wearing gold armlets, seated on a silver throne; walking haughtily, thinking proudly, speaking loftily to the crowd of servants, flatterers in his train, before an extravagant table, before the greetings of all who approach him in the public square, some rising from their seats, some going forth to meet him, some escorting him, some carrying staffs to provide security. When you see these rulers, preceded by a herald with an uplifted voice, when you see them terrorizing one and torturing another, confiscating this one's property and delivering that one to death, do not fear what you see, do not be dismayed by those who command that these things happen, do not let your imagination astound you. Take to heart that God molded the human being, dust from the earth. If he is something else, fear him, but if he is dust from the earth, despise him.

14 "And God molded the human being." The word "molded" does not show us straightaway some technical activity of God concerning the human. "God molded." So did he mold in the same way as those who mold clay figures? As those who cast bronze? But the molding of a statue and the modeling of plaster possess imitation as far as the outward surface. You have seen how statues are presented with a particular character. The statue of a soldier expresses courage, or the metal expresses a feminine disposition when it is modeled on a woman, or something else, which artistic skill is able through imitation to introduce through features of character.

God's molding is not of this kind, but he molded the human being, and his creating activity fashioned all things in depth, working from within. If I had sufficient leisure for this, I might show you the structure of the human being, and you would learn from yourself the wisdom of God concerning you; that in truth the human being is a small cosmos, and they are beautifully made who are honored by him with this name. How many studies have been devoted to this matter? The physiologies of the doctors, the observations of gymnastic trainers about the proportion or symmetry of the limbs in relation to each other or about the many muscles, all these things enter into the modeling of the human being. And from what source can I produce such a discourse as to enable me to say with exactitude those things encompassed in the word "molded"? As for things close at hand, even if I have not spoken of them, you know them.

15   God created you upright. He gave this special structure to you as distinct from the rest of the animals.

   Why?

   Because the activity he intended to give you is also special. For they are grazing animals, and they are structured in accord with the things toward which they aim by nature. The sheep was created to go to pasture, it has its head inclining downward, looking at the stomach and the parts below the stomach, since the fulfillment of happiness for these animals is filling the stomach and enjoying pleasure. But the human being no longer looks toward the stomach, but his head is lifted high toward things above, that he may look up to what is akin to him. His eyes do not incline toward the ground. Therefore do not make yourself go against nature; do not focus on earthly things but on heavenly things, where Christ is. "For if you are resurrected together with Christ," says Scripture, "seek the things above, where Christ is" [Col 3.1]. Thus you were molded. That which has been molded is a lesson about the purpose for which you were born. You were born that you might see God, not that your life might be dragged down on the earth, not that you might have the pleasure of beasts, but that you might achieve heavenly citizenship. Because of this, "The eyes of the wise are in his head" [Eccl 2.14], as wise Ecclesiastes says.

Who does not have eyes in his head?

"In the head" means to look at things on high. But one who does not look toward things on high but toward earthly things has eyes dragged down toward earth.

16   Moreover, the eyes are round, the head is placed on the shoulders without being pressed down, so that it may not be low; but it is placed on a noteworthy support, the neck. The head is high, and the eyes are twin gazes.

Why was one eye not enough for me?

Two eyes take each other's place, that the failure of one may have relief from the other. Then indeed the vision coming forth from one is weaker; but the stream converging from two sources becomes more vigorous. For the vision is added, it rests together with the support of the nose, and peeping out together, unites itself. For like some current, what is seen comes forth from each visible object, this from here, that from there; and coming forward it unites from what converges. And what is united becomes stronger.

What is the proof that it unites?

Do you not see that the elderly do not see things nearby? For then the vision, being divided, is weak, it does not see what is near; but where there is a convergence of vision, as if some flood of vision occurs, the grasp of things perceived becomes more vigorous.

And how many protections are around the eye?

There is an inner membrane, and this is not sufficient; for it could not be thick. If it were thick, it would be a curtain over the vision. It had to be transparent and light. Therefore one membrane is transparent, one is thin; the first is crystalline, the second is like horn. The covering one is stronger, the inner one lighter, that it may not obstruct the passage. The third is crystalline, that it might have in itself the imprint and the transparency of each.

The eyelid is a screen, a curtain and covering, and is a sort of dwelling place and fortress. The hand could cover the eye, but before the hand came, the eye would already have been obscured. But now the eyelid lies close by, placed above; at once it perceives the harm and puts forward the covering. Because of this the pupil also, placed under a covering, is not continually open to attack. The eye, alone of our organs, wishes to be untouched; it is veiled by the covering of the eyelid.

It is surrounded by lashes. Why?

That the entwining of the upper and lower eyelids may be more exact. For the lashes entwined with each other are a kind of fastening; therefore from a distance they stop the insects, and dust particles may prove unable to approach the pupil from all sides so as to obscure it. There is a particular protection because of the lashes surrounding us; the eye is adorned pleasantly by their outline, and at the same time this provides something useful.

The eyebrow is projected above as a kind of protuberance, so as to keep the vision straight.

What is the proof of this?

When you want to look at a distance, and you curve your hand and stretch it over your eyebrow, why do you do this? So that the vision's upward movement may not allow it to scatter, since it is straightened by the screen of the hand and directed forward, making the straightness of the vision more exact and vigorous. The passage of the vision is straightened by the screen of the hand. Therefore the eyebrows direct the eye straight and simultaneously prevent the sweat caused by labors from flowing in and becoming a hindrance to vision. Because of this the eyebrows fortify it like a wall.

What vinedresser can prepare the vine so well as to surround it with a wall so it is difficult to attack, and it is not assailable by the torrents alongside the field, as the Lord made the fortification of the eyebrows? Happily for us, he formed one outline conjoining what is divided on each side of the nose, so that the sweat which flows here and there may not cause any concern for the farmer. So he need not take his hand from the vine to wipe clean the sweat, but the sweat flows through its own channels. Long ago the Creator drew it away to be discarded, so that the eye could perform its own activity at the same time.

17   If we wanted to speak only of the aspects of ourselves skillfully wrought by God, the whole day would not be sufficient. But from this one example you get the idea of all the rest.

But since we are going on a certain necessary journey, accompany us with prayers, that as you are speedily preserved, we may also repay the debt of things remaining, by the grace of the Lord who has planned all things concerning us, who has created us by his own grace, that to him be the glory unto ages of ages. Amen.

Homily Explaining that
God Is Not the Cause of Evil

1   There are many kinds of teaching shown us through the holy singer David by the Spirit who acts in him. For at one time, as the prophet describes to us in full his own sufferings, and how he bears nobly the things befalling him, through his own example he leaves us a most manifest teaching of patient endurance, as when he says, "Lord, why have they multiplied who afflict me?" [Ps 3.2]. At another time he commends the great goodness of God and the swiftness of his help, which is granted to those who truly seek him, saying, "When I called, the God of my justice heard me" [Ps 4.2]; the words uttered by the prophet have the same meaning, which say, "When you are speaking, he will say, 'Behold, I am with you' " [Is 58.9]. That is, he did not call beforehand, and God's hearing anticipated the aim of the invocation. Again, offering supplications to God and entreaties, he teaches us in what manner it is proper for those who are in sin to propitiate God: "Lord, do not reprove me in your anger, nor punish me in your wrath" [Ps 6.2]. And in the twelfth Psalm he points out a certain lengthening of temptation in the words that say, "How long, Lord, will you forget me to the end?" [Ps 12.1]. Through this whole psalm he teaches us not to be downcast in afflictions but to await the great goodness of God, and to know that a certain providential ordering is granted to us through affliction, that the amount of torment brought upon each to prove him is proportionate to the faith present in him. Then when he has said, "How long, Lord, will you forget me to the end?" and, "How long will you turn away your

face from me?" [Ps 12.1], straightway he passes to the evil of the athe-
ists. When one of the little things in life gives offense to them, not
bearing the more troublesome circumstances, straightway they
become doubtful in their minds about whether there is a God who
is attentive to things in this world, whether he watches over each person's concerns, whether he distributes to each the things of which he
is worthy. Then when they truly endure ill-advised conditions for a
long time, they confirm in themselves the evil belief, and they declare
in their hearts that there is no God. "The fool says in his heart, 'There
is no God'" [Ps 13.1]. Moreover, as this enters into his mind, he then
moves freely through every sin. For if there is no overseer, if there is
nobody who repays each according to the merit of his actions, what
prevents oppression of the poor, murder of orphans, killing of wid-
ows and strangers, daring to do every profane practice, wallowing in
unclean and abominable passions and all bestial desires? Accordingly, after the psalm says, "There is no God," it adds, "They have
become corrupt and abominable in their practices" [Ps 13.1]. For one
cannot turn aside from the just path unless one's soul is ill through
forgetting God.

2   Why are the nations handed over to a reprobate mind, and why
do they do what is improper [Rom 1.28]? Is it not because they said,
"There is no God?" Why have they fallen into dishonorable passions,
as the females among them have changed the natural usage into
what is unnatural, while the males commit unseemly acts with males
[Rom 1.26]? Is it not because they have exchanged the glory of the
incorruptible God for the likeness of cattle and four-footed beasts
and reptiles [Rom 1.23]? Therefore he is a fool, truly deprived of his
mind and wisdom, who says, "There is no God." It is one like him,
who leaves undone nothing foolish, who also says that God is the
cause of evils. For I regard their sins as being of equal rank, since
both alike deny the Good One, the one saying absolutely that he does
not exist, while the other concludes that he is not good. For if he is
the cause of evils, clearly he is not good, so that in both cases there

is denial of God. Whence, then, he asks, are diseases? Whence untimely deaths? Whence the utter destruction of cities? Ship-wrecks, wars, pestilences? For these also are evils, he says, and all are creations of God. So do we have anything else other than God to blame for the things that occur? Now therefore, since we have arrived at this much-discussed question, as we bring the discussion to an appropriate starting point and make a further effort to state the problem precisely, let us attempt to explain the issue clearly and without confusion.

3   This one thing must be held firmly in our mind, that since we are a creation of the good God and are welded together by him, as he manages smaller and greater things concerning us, neither can we undergo anything that is not God's will, nor do we truly suffer any-thing that is hurtful unless it can be understood to bring us some-thing better. For deaths are from God; truly not every death is evil, except if one speaks of the death of the sinner, since his departure from here is the beginning of punishments in hell. And again, the evils in hell do not have God as their cause, but we cause them. For the beginning and root of sin is in us and in our self-determination. For it was possible for those abstaining from evil to suffer nothing terrible, but as for those enticed through pleasure into sin, to state the matter properly, do they not themselves become the cause of their sufferings? Moreover, what our senses perceive as evil is one thing, while what is evil in its own nature is another. What is evil by nature has been produced by us, namely injustice, licentiousness, folly, cowardice, envy, murder, poisoning, laziness, and passions akin to these, which defile the soul that has come into being according to the image of the Creator and have caused a shadow to pass over the soul's own beauty. On the contrary, we call what is toilsome and painful to our sense perception evil, bodily illness, and blows to the body, and lack of necessities, and disgrace, and financial setbacks, and loss of property. Each of these is brought to us by the wise and good Master for our advantage. For wealth is taken away from those

who have used it badly, thus destroying the instrument of injustice. He sends illness to those for whom it is more profitable to have their limbs constrained than to move unhindered toward sinning. Death is brought to those whose time of life is completed; from the beginning the just judgment of God has appointed this for each person, as he foresees from long before what is advantageous to each of us. Famines and droughts and floods are in a certain manner common blows to cities and nations, punishing the excess of evil. As, therefore, the physician is a benefactor even if he produces distress or pain in the body (for he fights the illness, not the sick person), so also God is good, who provides salvation to all, through particular punishments. And you do not accuse the physicians of any wrong in his cuttings and burnings and complete mutilations of the body; but rather you probably pay him money and you call him a savior, since he has produced illness in a small part of the body to prevent the suffering from spreading throughout the whole of it. But whenever you see a city fall down on its inhabitants in an earthquake, or a ship and its whole crew lost at sea, you do not hesitate to wag your tongue in blasphemy against the true Physician and Savior. And further, one must understand that there are moderate and curable illnesses of human beings, which are helped by care, but whenever the disease is shown to be too severe for treatment, it becomes necessary to cut off the part that has become useless, so that the illness does not continue and proceed to spread into the vital organs. Therefore, as the physician is not the cause of the surgery or the cautery, but the illness is, so also, as the obliteration of cities has its source in the excess of those who have sinned, God is acquitted of all blame.

4   Yet indeed if God is not the cause of evils, it is asked, in what sense has he said, "I fashion light and make darkness, I make peace and create evils" [Is 45.7]. And again, "There came down," Scripture says, "evils from the Lord upon the gates of Jerusalem" [Mic 1.12], and, "There are no evils in the city which the Lord did not make" [Am 3.6]. And in the great Song of Moses it says, "Behold, behold

that I am, and there is no God but me. I kill and I make to live, I will strike and I will heal" [Deut 32.39]. But to one who understands the mind of Scripture, none of these verses contains an accusation against God as a cause and creator of evils, for the one who says, "I fashion light and make darkness," presents himself as artisan of the creation through these things, not as a creator of evil. Therefore, that you may not consider one principle to be the cause of light, another of darkness, he has declared himself to be the Creator and Fashioner who has made the things that appear to be opposites. So do not seek one artisan of fire and another of water, nor one of air and another of earth, since they seem in a certain way to lie opposite to each other because of their contrasting properties. Through experiencing this very thing, some have previously turned toward polytheism.

Yet God makes peace and he creates evils. Certainly on the one hand he makes peace in you when through good teaching he pacifies your mind and reconciles the passions that rebel against the soul. On the other hand he creates evils, that is, he transforms them and brings improvement, so that they cease to be evils and participate in the nature of good. "Create in me a clean heart, O God" [Ps 50.12]. Do not make something now, but renew what has grown old through evils. And, "that he may make the two into one new human being" [Eph 2.15]. Here the word "make" means not that something is brought out of non-being, but that beings are transformed. And, "If anyone is in Christ, he is a new creation" [2 Cor 5.17]. And again, Moses says, "Is not he himself your Father who has acquired you, and made you, and created you?" [Deut 32.6]. For clearly here the "creation" placed after the "making" teaches us that the meaning of improvement has been assigned, as in many cases, to the term "creation." Therefore, when it says, "I make peace," it means that he makes peace out of things that create evils, that is he transforms them and brings improvement.

Yet even if you understand peace as the freedom from wars, and say that evils are the hardships that follow those who make war, service abroad, labors, sleeplessness, struggles, sweats, wounds, slaughters, conquests of cities, enslavements, abductions, the miseries of captives paraded as spectacles, and in a word all the sufferings that follow war, we say they occur by the just judgment of God, who allots punishment through wars to those deserving of chastisement. Or do you wish that Sodom had not been burnt to ashes after those wicked deeds? Or should Jerusalem not have been subdued, nor the temple laid waste, after the horrible insanity of the Jews against the Lord? Could these things have occurred justly in some other way, and not through the hands of the Romans, to whom the Jews, the enemies of their own life, betrayed our Lord? Therefore, there is a time when the evils of war are also approved justly for those who deserve them.

And the words, "I kill and I make to live," you can accept, if you like, in the obvious sense. For fear edifies the simpler people. "I will strike and I will heal." This also is understood as useful in the same sense. The blow produces fear, while the healing persuades you to love. Yet clearly a higher way of understanding these words can be found. "I kill" refers to sin, and "I make to live" refers to justice. "To the extent that our outer self is wasting away, our inner self is being renewed" [2 Cor 4.16]. He does not kill one person and make another to live, but through that which he kills he also gives life. And through that by which he strikes, he heals, in accord with what is read in the Proverb: "If you strike him with a rod, you deliver his soul from death" [Prov 23.14]. Therefore the flesh is struck that the soul may be healed, and sin is put to death that justice may be made alive. And the words, "There came down evils from the Lord upon the gates of Jerusalem," provide their own interpretation. What kind of evils? The clamor of chariots and horsemen. And when you hear, "There are no evils in the city that the Lord did not make," understand that the word "evils" names the bringing of evils upon sinners for the correction of their faults. "For I afflicted you," it says, "and I weakened you by hunger" [Deut 8.3], in order to do good to you, to prevent injustice from pouring forth without measure, just as a stream is held back by a strong wall and barricade.

5   For these things, disorders of cities and nations, droughts in the air and barrenness of the earth, the harsh calamities in the life of each, cut short the growth of evil. Therefore evils such as these come into being from God, and they stop true evils from coming into being. For the bodily sufferings and outward distresses have been invented to halt sin. Therefore God removes evil, and evil is not from God, since likewise the physician removes illness but does not produce it in the body. But razings of cities, earthquakes and floods, and destructions of armies, and shipwreck, and every occasion when many people are killed either by earth, or by sea, or by air, or fire, or by whatever cause it befalls, these happen for the correction of the survivors, as collective wickedness is corrected by a public flogging from God. So sin is evil in the proper sense, and it is especially worthy of the name of evil. It is brought about by our free choice, since it is up to us either to abstain from vice or to be wicked. But of the remaining evils, some are provided as contests to demonstrate courage, as when Job suffered the deprivation of his children, the disappearance of all his wealth at one pivotal moment, and the calamity of festering wounds. Other evils come as a remedy for sins, as when David endured the shame surrounding his house when a penalty was exacted for his unlawful desire. In addition we have observed another kind of horror brought about by the just judgment of God, to make more moderate those easily slipping toward sin, as when Dathan and Abiron were swallowed by the earth as clefts and chasms burst open for them. For they have not themselves become better by this kind of punishment (How could they, since they were going down to hell?), but those who remained have been made more moderate by their example. Thus also Pharaoh was thrown into the sea with his whole army. Thus the previous inhabitants of Palestine were obliterated.

Therefore, when the Apostle speaks of "vessels of wrath prepared for destruction" [Rom 9.22], let us not imagine that there is a kind of wicked preparation of Pharaoh, for then it would be more just to transfer the causality to the one preparing him. Rather, when you hear "vessel," understand that each of us has been made for something useful. It is as in a big house, where some vessels are of gold, some of silver, some of earthenware, and some of wood. The free choice of each provides the likeness in the material. The vessel of gold is one who is pure in character and without guile, while the silver is inferior in merits to that one. The earthenware is one earthly minded and fit to be crushed, and the wood is one prone to be defiled through sin and become fuel for eternal fire. Hence similarly the vessel of wrath is that which, like a jar, contains all the activity of the devil. Because of that which has come about in it due to the stench of decay it is no longer able to be of use but deserves only disappearance and destruction. For this reason, since it was necessary that Pharaoh be crushed, the prudent and wise manager of souls pursued him in a way that was seen all around and heard from afar, so that at least he would come to be of benefit to others through his sufferings, since he was himself incurable because of too much evil. And he hardened him by longsuffering and the delay of the punishment, increasing his evils so that as his wickedness grew to the farthest extreme, the justice of the divine judgment upon him would be manifest. Therefore as he was led from smaller blows to increasing plagues, he did not relent in his rebelliousness, but he despised the forbearance of God and by habit found training in the calamities inflicted on him. And thus he was not delivered by death until he submerged himself in the water, presuming in the arrogance of his heart to make the passage of the just, and thinking that the Red Sea would be passable for him as indeed it was for the people of God.

Therefore, having learned these things clearly from God, you can distinguish for yourself between the kinds of evil, and know which is real evil, namely sin, whose end is destruction, and what seems evil because it is painful to the senses but has a capacity for good, such as the distresses that bring about a cessation of sin, whose fruit is the eternal salvation of souls. Stop being displeased with divine providence. In short, do not maintain that God is the cause of evil's existence, nor imagine evil to have a subsistence of its own. For wickedness does not subsist as if it were a living being. Nor do we hold that its essence coexists in another subsistence. For evil is a privation of good. The eye was created, but blindness comes into being following the destruction of eyes. Therefore, if the eye did not have a perishable nature, blindness would not have a means of entry. Thus also evil is not in itself an existence but arises following the maiming of the soul. For neither is it ungenerated, as the impious argue, making the wicked of equal honor to the nature of good, if indeed both are without origin and have come into being from above, nor indeed is it generated. For if all things are of God, how is evil from good? For neither is the ugly from the beautiful, nor vice from virtue. Read the account of the [material] world's creation, and you will find there, "All things are good, and very good" [Gen 1.31]. Accordingly, evil was not created together with good. But neither was the intelligible creation, having come to be from the Fashioner, mixed with wickedness when brought into being. For if bodily things did not have evil co-created in themselves, how could the intelligible things, bearing such purity and holiness, have a common subsistence with evil? Yet indeed evil exists, and its activity shows that it is greatly poured forth in all of life. From what source, then, does it exist, one asks, if it is neither without origin nor created?

6   Let those who inquire about such matters be asked in turn, from what source are illnesses? From what source are the maimings of the body? For neither is illness ungenerated, nor is it the handiwork of God. But living beings were created with the bodily faculties suited to them according to nature, and brought into life complete in their limbs and organs, but they became ill through a perversion of what is according to nature. For a disruption of health occurs either because of a bad lifestyle or because of some other cause of illness. Therefore, God created the body, but not illness; and likewise God created the soul, but not sin. Rather, the soul is made evil through a perversion of what is according to nature.

But what was the good set before the soul? It was attentiveness to God and union with him through love. Once the soul has fallen away from this, it is made evil by various and manifold weaknesses. But for what reason is it entirely capable of receiving evil? Because of the impulse of free choice, especially befitting a rational nature. For having been freed from all necessity, and receiving self-determined life from the Creator, because it came into being according to the image of God, it understands the Good and knows his joy and possesses authority and power, abiding in the contemplation of the beautiful and the enjoyment of spiritual things, guarding carefully in itself the life according to nature. Yet it also had authority to turn away from the beautiful at any time. And this happened to it when it received a satiety of blessed delights and was as it were weighed down by a kind of sleepiness and sank down from things above, being mixed with the flesh through the disgraceful enjoyment of pleasures.

7   There was a time when Adam was set on high, not in place but by free choice, when, having just then been given life, he looked up toward heaven and became exceedingly glad at the things he saw. He greatly loved his Benefactor, who gave him the enjoyment of eternal life, enabled him to rest amid the delights of paradise, gave him authority like that of the angels, made his way of life the same as that of the archangels, and let him hear the divine voice. As he was protected in all these things by God and enjoyed the blessings belonging to him, he quickly became full of everything. And as it were becoming insolent through satiety, he preferred what appeared delightful to the fleshly eyes to the spiritual beauty and considered the filling of the stomach more valuable than the spiritual enjoyments. And immediately he was outside paradise and outside that blessed way of life, becoming evil not from necessity but from thoughtlessness. Because of this he also sinned through wicked free choice, and he died through the sin. "For the wages of sin is death" [Rom 6.25]. For to the extent that he withdrew from life, he likewise

drew near to death. For God is life, and the privation of life is death. Therefore Adam prepared death for himself through his withdrawal from God, in accord with what is written, "Behold, those who remove themselves from you are destroyed" [Ps 72.27]. Thus God did not create death, but we brought it upon ourselves by a wicked intention. To be sure, for the reason stated above, he did not prevent our dissolution, so that our weakness might not remain as immortal. It is like someone not allowing a leaky clay pot to be placed in fire [and hardened] until the weakness present in it has been completely mended through refashioning.

But why did we not have sinlessness in our structure, one may ask, so that the will to sin would not exist in us? Because indeed it is not when your household slaves are in bonds that you consider them well disposed, but when you see them willingly fulfill your wishes. Accordingly, God does not love what is constrained but what is accomplished out of virtue. And virtue comes into being out of free choice and not out of constraint. But free choice depends on what is up to us. And what is up to us is self-determined. Accordingly, the one who finds fault with the Creator for not fashioning us by nature sinless is no different from one who prefers the nonrational nature to the rational, and what lacks motion and impulse to what has free choice and activity. If indeed these points are a digression, it was necessary to say them, lest falling into an abyss of arguments, you remain deprived of the things you most desire and also deprived of God. Therefore, let us stop correcting the Wise One. Let us stop seeking what is better than the things that have come from him. For if indeed the detailed principles of what he has planned escape us, let this belief be present in your souls, namely that nothing evil comes into being from the Good One.

8   But what also comes to mind following our sequence of thought is the question about the devil. From where does the devil come, if evils are not from God? What then shall we say? That the same argument that was offered regarding wickedness in the human being also

helps us in this inquiry. But for what reason is the human being evil?
Because of his freedom of choice. For what reason is the devil evil?
For the same reason the devil possesses a life endowed with self-
determination, and the authority rests in himself either to remain
with God or to become estranged from the good. Gabriel is an angel,
and he stood by God continually. Satan is an angel, and he fell away
from his proper place entirely. The free choice of the one kept him
in things above, and the self-determination of the other threw him
down. For the one could have become an enemy, and the other need
not have fallen, but the one was preserved by his insatiable love of
God, while his withdrawal from God showed the other as worthless.
Evil consists in estrangement from God. With a small turning of the
eye, we are either facing the sun or facing the shadow of our own
body. Thus one who looks upward easily finds illumination, but for
one who turns toward the shadow darkening is inevitable. Thus the
devil is wicked because he possesses wickedness by free choice, not
through a natural opposition to the good.

Why does he fight against us? Because, being a receptacle of all
evils, he also accepted the disease of malice and envied our honor.
For he could not bear our life free from pain in paradise. With tricks
and contrivances he thoroughly deceived the human being, and,
misusing the desire he had for likeness to God to deceive him, he
showed him the tree and promised that through eating it he would
be made like God. "For if you eat," he said, "you will be like gods,
knowing good and evil" [Gen 3.5]. Accordingly, he was not fashioned
as our enemy, but out of jealousy he stood against us in enmity. For
seeing himself thrown down from among the angels, he could not
bear to see the earthly one lifted through progress to the rank of the
angels.

9   Therefore, since he became an enemy, God fostered our opposition to him. Because of this he spoke to him through the animal
who served him and directed this threat toward it: "I will place
enmity between you and her seed" [Gen 3.15]. For reconciliation

with the Evil One is harmful, since there is a law that friendship grows from likeness between those who are united. Therefore, it is rightly said, "Bad companions ruin good morals" [1 Cor 15.33]. For in disease-producing regions, like the air breathed little by little, an unnoticed illness is produced in the inhabitants. Similarly, the habitual association with petty worthless things lets great evils drop into the soul, even if the harm escapes immediate perception. For this reason the enmity toward the serpent is irreconcilable. But if the instrument is deserving of such hatred, how much is it proper for us to be at enmity with the one acting in it?

Yet, one may also ask, for what reason was the tree in paradise, through which the devil's attack on us was about to take place? For if he had not had the bait for his deceit, how would he have led us on through the disobedience into death? Because there needed to be a commandment to test our obedience. For this reason there was a tree abundantly bearing ripe fruit, that in abstaining from the pleasure, as we manifested the goodness of self-restraint, we might justly be worthy of the crowns of perseverance. But there followed from the eating not only disobedience of the commandment, but also the full knowledge of nakedness. "For they ate," it says, "and their eyes were opened, and they knew that they were naked" [Gen 3.7]. But it was necessary that they not know their nakedness, that the mind of the human being might not turn toward the fulfillment of lesser needs, to consider clothes for himself and relief from nakedness, and through concern for the flesh be entirely dragged away from gazing intently toward God.

Yet for what reason were clothes not immediately fashioned for him? Because these things were not fitting either by nature or by art. For on the one hand they belong by nature to the nonrational animals, such as feathers, and hair, and thick skins, either to cover them in winter or to enable them to bear burning heat. In these coverings nothing has distinguished them one from another, for they all have a nature of equal honor. But it was fitting for the human being, according to the intensity of his love for God, to be given instead things surpassing these good things. But the things invented through devotion to art promote business, which is especially to be avoided as harmful to the human being. Therefore also the Lord, recalling us to the life in paradise, expels anxiety from our soul, saying, "Do not be anxious about your lives, what you will eat, neither about your bodies, what you will wear" [Mt 6.25]. Therefore it is not appropriate for Adam to have coverings either by nature or by art. But other clothes had been prepared, had he shown virtue, those coming by the gift of God to blossom for the human being, certain shining garments flashing forth like those of the angels, exceeding the varieties of flowers and the radiance and brilliance of the stars. So for this reason the clothes were not immediately given to him, since as prizes for virtue they were held in store for the human being, if he had not beforehand yielded to the abuse of the devil.

Accordingly, the devil has remained as our opponent because of the fall that came upon us due to his abuse long ago. So the Lord has planned for us wrestling with him so that we would wrestle through obedience and triumph over the adversary. If only he had not set out to become a devil but remained at the post at which in the beginning he was stationed by the Commander! But since he became a rebel, he is an enemy of God, and also an enemy of the human being who has come into existence according to the image of God. For on this account he hates humankind, because he also fights against God, and he hates us both as belonging to the Master and as likenesses of God. Therefore we were joined in battle against his wickedness as a training exercise for our souls by the one who plans human affairs with wisdom and foreknowledge, as a physician uses the viper's poison to make medicines for healing.

Who then was the devil? What was his rank? What was his dignity? And why in short has he been named Satan? He is Satan, therefore, because he stands opposite to the good, for this is what the Hebrew word means, as we have learned in the Book of Kings: "For," it says, "the Lord raised up an adversary [literally, a "satan"] against Solomon, Hadad king of the Syrians" [1 Kg 11.14]. And he is a devil since he himself both collaborates in our sin and becomes our accuser, he rejoices in our destruction while he makes an example of us for the things we have done. And his nature is bodiless, according to the Apostle, who says, "Our wrestling is not with flesh and blood, but with the spirits of wickedness" [Eph 6.12]. And his honor is that of a ruler. "Against the rulers," he says, "and the authorities, and the cosmic powers of darkness" [ibid.]. And his place of rule is in the air, as the same epistle says, "Against the ruler of the powers of the air, the spirit who now works in the sons of disobedience" [Eph 2.2]. For this reason also he is called ruler of the world, since his rule surrounds the earth. And thus the Lord says, "Now is the judgment of this world, now the ruler of this world will be thrown out" [Jn 12.31]. And again, "The ruler of this world is coming, and in me you will find nothing" [Jn 14.36].

10   Yet since it has been said regarding the devil's army, "They are spirits of wickedness in the heavenly places" [Eph 6.12], one must understand that Scripture often says "heaven" when it means the air, as in "the birds of heaven" [Mt 6.26], and, "they go up into the heavens" [Ps 107.26], that is, they are raised up high in the air. For this reason also the Lord says, "I saw Satan falling as lightning from heaven" [Lk 10.18], that is, he fell from his own realm and came down, that he might be trampled under foot by those who have hoped in Christ. For he has given power to his own disciples to trample on serpents and scorpions and on all the power of the enemy [Lk 10.19]. Therefore, since his wicked tyranny is overthrown, and the region surrounding the earth is cleansed through the passion of the Savior, who makes peace between things on earth and things in the heavens, henceforth the kingdom of heaven is proclaimed to us. John says, "The kingdom of heaven has come near" [Mt 3.2], while the Lord proclaims the good news of the kingdom everywhere. And still earlier the angels shout, "Glory to God in the highest, and peace on earth" [Lk 2.14], and those rejoicing at the entrance of our Lord into Jerusalem cry, "Peace in heaven, and glory in the highest" [Lk

19.38]. And in short, the victorious have tens of thousands of voices. They are manifested as purified from the enemy to the end. For not one wrestling or contest will remain for us on high, nor will anyone be set against us and turn us aside from the blessed life. But we will have an uninterrupted existence without pain and enjoy the tree of life, from which we were prevented from partaking since the beginning through the plot of the serpent. "For God appointed the flaming sword to guard the way to the tree of life" [Gen 3.24]. Passing it unhindered, may we enter into the enjoyment of good things in Christ Jesus our Lord, to whom be glory and dominion unto the ages. Amen.

Homily against Anger

1 When medical precepts are to the point and accord with the art's teachings, their usefulness is demonstrated above all from experience; likewise with spiritual injunctions, above all when the precepts receive testimony from their outcome, then they are manifest as wise and useful for the correction of life and the perfection of those who comply with them. For we have heard Proverbs explicitly declare, "Anger destroys even the prudent" [Prov 15.1], and we have also heard the apostolic injunction, "Put away from you all anger and temper and clamor, with all malice" [Eph 4.31], and the Lord's saying that one who is angry without purpose at his brother is subject to judgment [Mt 5.22]. Now, when we have come to experience this passion, not arising in ourselves but assaulting us from outside like some unexpected tempest, then above all we discover the excellence of the divine precepts. When we make space for the anger, like an outlet for a violent river, while quietly observing the undignified confusion of those overpowered by the passion, we discover from their actions that these words are to the point: "An angry man is not dignified" [Prov 11.25].

For whenever, once reason has been pushed aside, the passion takes control of the soul for itself, it makes the human being entirely like a wild beast; it does not allow him to be a human being, since he no longer has the help of reason. For as venom is in venomous animals, so temper becomes in those who are provoked. They are maddened like dogs, they strike like scorpions, they bite like snakes. Scripture also acknowledges this in calling those ruled by this passion by the name of wild beasts, to whom they have made themselves

81

akin through evil. For it calls them dumb dogs [Is 56.10], and snakes, a generation of vipers [Mt 23.33], and the like. For those prepared to destroy each other and harm those of their own kind would be appropriately counted among the wild beasts and venomous animals, in whom is present by nature an irreconcilable hatred toward human beings.

Because of anger tongues are unbridled and lips are unguarded; unrestrained hands, outrages, reproaches, slanders, blows, and other such things that cannot be numbered, are offspring of the passions of anger and temper. Through temper also a sword is sharpened; a human hand dares to kill a human being. Through this brothers have become ignorant of each other, and parents and children have forgotten their natural bond. For angry persons are first ignorant of themselves, then indeed of all their friends as well. For as mountain torrents rushing together toward the valleys sweep away whatever is in their path, so the violent and ungovernable attacks of angry people likewise sweep through everything. Those whose temper is aroused respect neither gray hairs, nor virtuous life, nor close kinship, nor favors previously received, nor anything else worthy of honor. Temper is a kind of short-lived insanity. Often they even rush to do manifest harm to themselves in their zeal for revenge, heedless of their own concerns. For as if stung on all sides by a gadfly by the memory of those who have grieved them, as their temper struggles and leaps within them, they do not desist until either they have done some harm to those who have provoked them, or perhaps also received some, as may happen, as often objects that are smashed violently suffer greater damage than they cause when shattered against hard bodies.

2   Who could adequately describe the evil, how those with quick tempers, having fastened on a chance pretext, shouting and furious, attack no less than some shameless venomous beast? Such a person does not stop until great and incurable harm is done, as if a bubble of anger bursts and boiling, seething hot phlegm pours out. For

neither a sword's edge, nor fire, nor anything else frightening, is sufficient to hold back the soul driven insane by anger; any more, perhaps, than they hold back those subject to the demons, from whom angry people differ in nothing, either in the appearance or in the disposition of their soul. For in those who long for revenge, the blood boils around the heart as if stirred up and blustering because of a raging fire. Bursting forth to appear visibly, it shows the angry person with an appearance different from the one customary and familiar to all, as if it were exchanged for some mask on stage. Those near him do not recognize in his eyes their usual expression; but his gaze is frenzied and fire is in his eyes. He sharpens his teeth like a boar going into battle. His face is livid and suffused with blood, his swollen body is heavy, his blood vessels burst. His breathing rushes wildly, driven by the storm within. His voice is harsh and strained to the uttermost, and his speech is inarticulate, pouring forth heedlessly, proceeding without sequence or order or clarity.

But whenever anger becomes implacable, like a flame with abundant fuel, and holds tight to provocations, then indeed the spectacle is indescribable and unbearable to behold. His hands are lifted against his kinsfolk and all the limbs of his body attack, while his feet leap mercilessly upon the most vital organs, and everything at hand becomes a weapon for the madness. And if such persons also find an equal wickedness fighting against them from the opposing side, another anger and a similar insanity, then indeed they come to blows. They then inflict on each other and themselves suffer such things as perchance those under the command of such a demon are to suffer. For maiming of limbs or even death are often the prizes of anger that those fighting carry away. One started to do violence unjustly and the other repaid it; the second inflicted harm in return, the first did not submit. And the body is cut asunder by blows, while the temper removes the perception of pain. For they do not have time for the perception of what they have suffered, since the whole of their soul has been moved toward revenge against those who have grieved them.

3   Do not then cure the evil with evil, nor attempt to outdo each other in such matters. For in contests for superiority in wickedness the victor is more miserable, since he departs having the greater sin. Therefore, do not become one who pays an evil debt in full, nor take out a wicked loan by greater wickedness. Has someone insulted you in anger? Stop the evil by silence. But you, as if receiving the stream of that person's anger into your own heart, imitate the wind, repaying by blowing back what it has borne to you. Do not use your enemy as a teacher, and as for what you hate, do not emulate this. Do not, as it were, become a mirror of the one prone to anger, showing the likeness of that person in yourself. He has turned red. But are you not the color of wine? His eyes are bloodshot. But, tell me, do yours look calm? His voice is harsh. Is yours gentle? The echo in the desert does not shout back as clearly to one who speaks loudly as the insults turn back against the abuser. Rather, the echo comes back the same while the abuse returns with something added. For what sorts of things do insulters say to each other? One says the other is an insignificant person born of an insignificant person; the other in return calls him a slave born of a slave in the household. One says "poor laborer," the other says "tramp." One says "stupid," the other says "crazy," until their insults, like arrows, run out. Then, when all the abuse of the tongue has been hurled, then in addition they proceed to avenge themselves through actions. For temper incites fighting, and fighting gives birth to abuse, and abuse to blows, and blows to wounds, and often wounds to death.

From the very beginning let us stop the evil, removing the anger from our souls by every contrivance. For thus we could excise the greatest number of evils together with this passion, since it is a kind of root and source. Has someone abused you? Bless him. Has he struck you? Endure it. Does he spit on you and regard you as nothing? Then accept this thought about yourself, that you were taken from the earth, and you will return to the earth again [Gen 3.19]. For one who applies this concept to himself beforehand, will find all dishonor to be less than the truth. For thus indeed you will provide your enemy no means of revenge, you will show yourself invulnerable to the abuse, and you will procure for yourself a great crown of perseverance, making the other's insanity a starting point for your own philosophy. So, if you listen to me, you will even add freely to the insults. Does he say you are insignificant, and lower class, and a nobody from nowhere? Then say you are yourself earth and ashes. You are not more majestic than our father Abraham, who called himself these things [Gen 18.27]. Does he call you stupid and a beggar and worthy of nothing? Then say that you are yourself a "worm" [Ps 22.6], and born from a dunghill, as David's words say. To these examples add also the goodness of Moses. When abused by Aaron and Miriam, he did not accuse them before God but prayed for them [Num 12.1ff]. Would you not choose to be a disciple of such men, who are friends of God and blessed, rather than of those filled with the spirit of wickedness?

When you are stirred by the temptation to abuse, consider that you are being tested as to whether through longsuffering you will come near to God, or through anger run away toward the adversary. Give your thoughts the opportunity to choose the good portion. For you will either help that person somehow through your example of meekness, or exact a more severe vengeance through disdain. For what could become more painful to your enemy, than to see his enemy as above insults? Do not overturn your own purpose, and do not appear to be easily accessible to those who insult you. Let him bark at you ineffectually; let it burst upon himself. For the one who strikes one who feels no pain takes vengeance on himself, for neither is his enemy repaid, nor is his temper assuaged. Likewise, the person reproaching one unaffected by abuse is unable to find relief for his passion. On the contrary, as I have said, he is indeed cut to the heart. Moreover, in these circumstances, what sorts of things will each of you be called? He is abusive, but you are magnanimous; he is prone to anger and hard to bear, but you are longsuffering and meek. He will change his mind about the things he said, but you will never repent of your virtue.

4   Why must I say so many things? The abuse shuts him out of the
kingdom of heaven, "for abusers will not inherit the kingdom of
God" [1 Cor 6.10]; but your silence prepares the kingdom, "for he
who perseveres until the end, that one will be saved" [Mt 10.22]. But
when you take revenge and oppose the abuse by equaling it, what
will you say in your defense? Is it enough that he provoked you? And
does that make you worthy of pardon? For the fornicator who trans-
fers the blame to his girlfriend, as having greatly enticed him toward
the sin, is no less worthy of condemnation. There are neither crowns
without opponents, nor defeats without adversaries. Listen to
David, who says, "When the sinner stood against me," not "I was provoked," or "I took revenge," but "I was mute and humbled, and I kept
silence from good things" [Ps 38.2–3, LXX]. But you are provoked by
the abuse since you consider it rude, bad, crass; yet you imitate it as
good. For behold, you have the same passion that you condemn. Are
you anxious to look down on another's evil? Or do you regard your
own disgraceful conduct as nothing? Are insults wicked? Flee from
imitating them. For indeed the fact that another started it does not
suffice to excuse you. Therefore, it is more just, as I myself am persuaded, even if his irritation is greater, since he did not have an
example of self-control; but you, seeing the ugliness of the angry
person, did not guard yourself against taking on his likeness, but are
irritated and annoyed and angry in return; and your passion
becomes an excuse for the one who started it. For by the things you
do yourself, you release him from guilt, and you condemn yourself.
For if temper is wicked, why did you not turn away from the evil?
But if it is worthy of pardon, why are you annoyed at the bad-tem-
pered person? So, if you came second to the angry exchange, this is
no advantage to you. For in wrestling matches, it is not the one who
moves first in a bout but the one who wins that is crowned. Accordingly, not only one who initiates something terrible, but also one
who follows a wicked leader toward sin, is condemned.

Suppose he calls you a poor laborer. If he speaks truly, admit the
truth; but if he lies, what are his words to you? Neither be filled with

conceit about praise that goes beyond the truth, nor be aggravated over insults that do not apply to you. Do you not see how arrows naturally pierce through hard and rigid objects, but their force is blunted by soft and yielding objects? Consider indeed that the power of abuse is of the same kind. One who resists it receives it into himself, while one who yields and withdraws dissolves by his gentleness of character the wickedness brought against him.

But why does the name "poor" trouble you? Remember your own nature, that you came naked into the world and will leave it naked [Job 1.21]. What is more poor than a naked person? You have heard nothing terrible, unless you claim what has been said as your own. Was anyone ever carried off to prison because of poverty? It is not shameful to be poor, but it is shameful not to bear the poverty nobly. Remember the Master, who "being rich, became poor for our sake" [2 Cor 8.9]. If you are called foolish and stupid, recall the Judean insults through which the true Wisdom was abased: "You are a Samaritan, and you have a demon" [Jn 8.48]. So if you act angry, you have confirmed the reproaches; for what is more foolish than anger? If you remain without anger, you shame the one insulting you, showing self-control through your actions.

Have you been struck? So also was the Lord. Have you been spat upon? So also was our Master. For, "he did not turn away his face from the shame of spitting" [Is 50.6]. Were you falsely accused? So also was the Judge. Did they tear off your garment? They also stripped my Lord and divided his clothes among themselves [Mt 27.31, 35]. You have not yet been condemned, you have not yet been crucified. Many things are lacking to you, if you would overtake him through imitation.

5   Let each of these things enter into your mind, and let them hold back the flames. For by preparing and predisposing ourselves beforehand through such reflections, we stop the leaping and throbbing of our heart and bring back our thoughts to steadiness and calm. This also, then, is what was said by David, that "I am prepared

and am not troubled" [Ps 119.60]. Accordingly, it is necessary to hold back the frantic and passion-stricken movement of the soul by remembering the examples of blessed men: how meekly the great David bore the raving violence of Shimei. For he did not give opportunity to the movement of anger, but redirecting his thought toward God, he said, "The Lord told Shimei to curse David" [2 Sam 16.10]. Therefore, upon hearing himself called a man of blood, a lawless man, he did not become aggravated by this but humbled himself, accepting the insults as if he deserved them. Strip away from yourself these two attitudes: neither consider yourself worthy of great things, nor regard another human being as greatly inferior to you in worth. For then our temper will never rise up against the dishonors that are brought upon us.

It is terrible for one who has benefited from good deeds and is indebted for great favors to be ungrateful and besides this to begin inflicting insults and dishonors. It is terrible, but more for the one doing it than for the one who suffers the evil. Let him insult you, but do not yourself inflict insults. Let what is said be an athletic school to train you in philosophy. If you have not been bitten, you are not wounded. But if indeed you suffer something in your soul, keep what causes pain within yourself. For the Psalmist says, "My heart is troubled within me" [Ps 143.47], that is, he did not let the passion pass to the outside but calmed it, as a wave is broken on the beach. Quiet for me your howling and raging heart. Let your passions respect the presence of reason in you, like a disorderly child at the coming of a respected man.

How, then, can we flee the damage caused by anger? We can persuade temper not to act before thought, but let us first take care that it never runs ahead of reason; let us keep it like a horse under a yoke, and let it obey reason as if it were a kind of bridle, never stepping outside its own place, but being led by reason wherever it guides it. Further, the soul's faculty of temper is useful to us in many of the acts of virtue. When like a soldier who has placed his arms in the custody of his commander, it readily offers help in what is ordered, it can perhaps be an ally to reason against sin. For the temper is a sinew of the soul, producing vigor in it for the accomplishment of good actions. When the soul is relaxed through pleasure, as when iron is hardened by tempering, this faculty leads it from being soft and slack to become austere and courageous. If your temper is not roused against the Evil One, you will not be able to hate him as much as he deserves. For I hold that it is necessary to have equal zeal for the love of virtue and for the hatred of sin. For this above all temper is useful. Whenever like a dog beside a shepherd it follows the rational faculty closely, it remains meek and tame toward those helping it, and readily available at the call of reason, while it is savage toward the strange voice and face, even if he seems to provide a service, but bows down when called by a companion or friend. The cooperation of the faculty of temper with the prudent part of the soul is most excellent and appropriate. For such a person will be irreconcilable and implacable toward things plotted against him, never accepting fondness toward what is harmful, but like a wolf ever howling and tearing to pieces the proposed pleasure. Such indeed is the usefulness of temper for those who know how to handle it.

For by the way it is used each of the other faculties also becomes either evil or good for the one who possesses it. As for the soul's faculty of desire, one who uses it for the enjoyment of the flesh and the consumption of impure pleasure is disgusting and licentious, while one who turns it toward the love of God and the longing for eternal good things is enviable and blessed. And again, as for the rational faculty, one who handles it well is prudent and intelligent, while one who sharpens his mind for the harm of his neighbor is a worker of mischief and evil.

6   Therefore, let us not make the faculties given us for salvation by the Creator into starting points of sin for ourselves. So also, indeed, the temper, moved when it is necessary and as it is necessary, produces courage and perseverance and self-restraint; but when acting against right reason it becomes insanity. For this reason also the

Psalm advises, "Be angry, but do not sin" [Ps 4.5]. And the Lord threatens judgment for those who are angered without purpose [Mt 5.22], but he does not reject the use of anger for things that are necessary, as a medicine. For the words, "I will place enmity between you and the serpent" [Gen 3.15], and "Be enemies of the Midianites" [Num 25.17], teach us to use temper as a weapon. For this reason Moses, the meekest of all people [Num 12.3], when punishing idolatry, placed weapons in the hands of the Levites for the slaughter of their brothers. He said, "Let each put his sword on his thigh, and go through from gate to gate, and return through the encampment; and let each kill his brother, and each his neighbor, and each the one near him" [Ex 32.27]. And a little later he says, "You have consecrated your hands today to the Lord, each in his son, and in his brother, that a blessing may be given to you" [Ex 32.29, LXX]. And what made Phineas just? Was it not his just anger against the fornicators? He, being very kind and gentle, when he saw that the fornication of Zambri and the Midianite woman had become open and shameless, and they did not hide the unseemly sight of their shame, did not hold back but used his temper for a needful purpose, driving his javelin through them both [Num 25.6–8]. And did not Samuel, when Agag the king of Amalek was kept alive by Saul contrary to the command of God, in just anger lead him forward and slaughter him [1 Sam 15.33]? So, often temper becomes a helper in good acts. And Elijah the zealot killed four hundred and fifty men, priests of shame, and four hundred men, priests of the groves, who ate at Jezebel's table, through considered and prudent temper, for the benefit of all Israel [1 Kgs 18.22–40].

But you are angry at your brother without purpose. For how is it not without purpose when one acts because the other provokes him? And you act like dogs who bite the stones when they cannot reach the one throwing them. The one acted upon is to be given compassion, the one acting is to be hated. Redirect your temper onto the murderer of human beings, the father of lies, the worker of sin; but sympathize also with your brother, because if he continues in sin, with the devil he will be delivered up to eternal fire.

Yet as temper and anger are different words, so also their meanings differ greatly from each other. For temper is a certain kind of heating and quick rising in steam of passion; but anger is an abiding sorrow and lasting impulse toward vengeance against the wrongdoers, as if the soul lusts for requital. Therefore it is necessary to know that human beings offend through both dispositions, either moved insanely and capriciously by provocations, or deceitfully and treacherously lying in wait for those who grieved them. We must guard against both these errors.

7   How, then, can the passion avoid being directed toward what it must avoid? How? It can if you are taught beforehand the humility which the Lord both prescribed in word and modeled in action, at one time saying, "Let the one who wishes to be first among you be last of all" [cf. Mt 9.35], and at another time, meek and unmoved, bearing with the one who struck him [Jn 18.22–23]. For the Maker and Master of heaven and earth, who is worshiped by all the intelligible and sense-perceptible creation, who "upholds all things by the word of his power" [Heb 1.8], did not send him alive into Hades, with the earth cleft beneath the impious one. Rather, he admonished and taught, "If I have spoken evilly, bear witness regarding the evil; but if I have spoken well, why do you strike me?" [Jn 18.23] For if you have become accustomed to being last of all in accord with the commandment of the Lord, when will you be irritated at having your dignity affronted? When a small child abuses you, the insults are an occasion for laughter; and when one driven out of his mind by inflammation of the brain speaks words of disdain, you think him worthy of compassion rather than hatred. Thus the movement of grief is engendered not by the insulting words but by our arrogance toward the one who has abused us and the fantasy each one of us has about himself. So if you put aside from your mind both of these, the noise of the words hurled at you will appear instead as an empty echo. Therefore, "Cease from anger, and leave behind temper" [Ps 37.8], that you may escape the judgment against anger, which "is

revealed from heaven upon all the impiety and injustice of human beings" [Rom 1.18]. For if by prudent thought you could cut out the bitter root of temper, you would remove with it many of the passions that begin from this source. For deceit and suspicion and faithlessness and malice and treachery and rashness, and the whole swarm of such wickednesses, are offshoots of this evil. Therefore, indeed, let us not bring to ourselves so great an evil. It is sickness of soul, darkening of thoughts, estrangement from God, ignorance of kinship, cause of conflict, fullness of misfortunes, a wicked demon coming to birth in our very souls. It is indeed as if a certain shameless inhabitant has taken possession beforehand of our inner self and closed the entrance to the Holy Spirit. For where enmity, strife, temper, quarreling, contentiousness and never-silent clamor are produced in the soul, there the Spirit of meekness does not rest. But let us listen to the advice of the blessed Paul and put away from us all anger and temper and clamor with all malice [Eph 4.31], and become kind and compassionate to each other, awaiting the blessed hope promised to the meek. For "blessed are the meek, for they will inherit the earth" [Mt 5.5], in Christ Jesus our Lord, to whom be glory and dominion unto the ages. Amen.

Homily on the Words
"Be Attentive to Yourself"

1   God who has created us has given us the use of language, that we may reveal the plans of our heart to each other and through our shared nature we may each give a share to our neighbor, as if from some treasury, showing forth our intentions from what lies hidden in our heart. For if we spent our lives with naked soul, we would immediately communicate with each other through our thoughts; but since our soul is concealed under veils of flesh as it produces thoughts, words and names are necessary to make public the things lying in the depth. Accordingly, since when our thought takes meaningful voice, as if carried in a ferry by our discourse, crossing the air it passes from the speaker to the hearer; and if it finds the sea calm and quiet, the discourse comes to anchor in the ears of the students as if in tranquil harbors untroubled by storms; but if as a kind of rough upsurge the clamor of the hearers blows adversely, it will be dissolved as it is shipwrecked in the air. Therefore make it calm for the discourse through silence. For perhaps something may appear useful, having things you can take with you. The word of truth is hard to catch and is easily able to escape those who do not examine it attentively, so the Spirit directs that it be brief and modest, to signify much in a few words, and through conciseness be easy to retain in the memory. For indeed the excellence proper to discourse is neither to hide the things signified in obscurity, nor to be redundant and empty, turning in all directions while overflowing randomly.

So what we have just read from the books of Moses is truly of this kind, which all of you who are diligent have remembered, unless possibly through brevity it has escaped your notice. The reading is as follows: "Be attentive to yourself, lest an unlawful word come to be hidden in your heart" [Deut 15.9]. We human beings are easily led toward sins of the mind. Therefore he who has formed our hearts individually, knowing that the greatest part of sin is accomplished in impulse through what is in our intention, has prescribed purity in our directive faculty as primary for us. For that by which we most readily sin was worthy of the most guarding and care. For as the physicians with greater foresight safeguard the weaker parts of bodies by precautionary advice ahead of time, so the universal protector and true physician of souls, who knows most of all where we are more liable to slide toward sin, has anticipated this with stronger guarding. For actions done through the body need time and opportunity and labors and co-workers and other requirements. But the movements of the mind operate timelessly, are completed without weariness, are constructed effortlessly, and are convenient on every occasion. Perhaps someone haughty who looks down on propriety, though clothed in the outward appearance of sobriety and sitting among many who call him blessed for his virtue, has run away in his mind to the place of sin in a hidden movement of his heart. He sees in imagination the things he seeks, he again imprints there some indecent liaison, and entirely within the secret workshop of the heart he paints a clear picture of the pleasure for himself. He has accomplished the sin inwardly and is without witness, unknown to all, until there comes the revelation of the hidden things of darkness and the disclosure of the intentions of hearts. Therefore be on guard lest at any time there come a lawless hidden word in your heart [Deut 15.9]. For one who looks at a woman with desire has already committed adultery in his heart [Mt 5.28]. Hence the actions of the body are impeded by many things, but those who sin by an intention brought about by the swiftness of thoughts still have the sin. Therefore, where the sharp point of transgression is, a safeguard has swiftly been given to us. For Scripture has testified, "lest at any time there come a lawless hidden word in your heart." However, let us return to the starting point of our discourse.

2   "Be attentive to yourself," it says. Each of the animals by nature has from the God who has constructed all things the resources to guard its own structure. And you would find, if you observed carefully, that most of the nonrational animals have without training an aversion to what is harmful, and again by a certain natural attraction they hasten toward the enjoyment of beneficial things. Therefore also God who is educating us has given us this great precept, that as this comes to them by nature, it comes to us by the help of reason, and as they are set right without reflection, we may accomplish this through the attentive and continuous care of thoughts. And guarding strictly the resources given us by God, let us flee sin as the nonrational animals flee harmful foods but pursue justice as they pursue nourishing grass. So be attentive to yourself, that you may be able to distinguish what is harmful from what is healthful. But attentiveness is of two kinds: on the one hand we can gaze intently with the bodily eyes at visible things, and on the other hand by its noetic faculty the soul can apply itself to the contemplation of incorporeal things. If we say that the precept refers to the activity of the eyes, immediately we would find it to be impossible. For how could one grasp the whole of oneself with one's eye? For neither can the eye be used to see itself, nor to reach the head, nor to see the back, nor the face, nor the arrangement of the internal organs deep within. Now it is impious to say that the precepts of the Spirit are impossible. It remains therefore to hear what is prescribed as applying to the activity of the mind. Be attentive to yourself, that is, observe yourself carefully from every side. Let the eye of your soul be sleepless to guard yourself. You walk in the midst of snares [Sir 9.13]. Hidden traps have been set by the enemy in many places. Therefore observe everything, "that you may be saved like a gazelle from traps and like a bird from snares" [Prov 6.5]. For because of keenness of sight the gazelle is not taken

by the traps, whence also it gives its name to its own sharp-sighted-
ness [an untranslatable play on words]; and the bird by lightness of
wing ascends higher than the plots of the hunters, when it is alert.
Therefore, see that you do not show yourself as worse than the nonrational animals in guarding yourself, lest when caught in the snares
you become prey to the devil, taken captive by him into his will [2
Tim 2.26].

3   Be attentive, then, to yourself, that is, neither to what is yours
nor to what is around you, but be attentive only to yourself. For we
ourselves are one thing, and what is ours is another, and the things
around us are another. Thus we are the soul and the mind, through
which we have come into being according to the image of the Creator, but the body is ours and the sense perceptions through it, while
around us are possessions, skills, and the other equipment of life.
What then does the Word say? Do not be attentive to the flesh, nor
pursue its good in every manner, health and beauty and enjoyment
of pleasures and long life, nor admire wealth and reputation and
power. As for those things that are of service to you in this tempo-
rary life, do not regard them as great. Through concern about these
things do not neglect the life that comes first for you, but be attentive to yourself, that is, to your soul. Adorn it and take care of it, so
that all the filth befalling it from wickedness may be removed
through attention, and all the shame due to evil may be cleansed
away, but adorn and brighten it with all the beauty that comes from
virtue. Examine what sort of being you are. Know your own nature,
that your body is mortal but your soul is immortal, and that our life
is twofold in kind. One kind is proper to the flesh, quickly passing
by, while the other is akin to the soul, not admitting of circumscrip-
tion. Therefore be attentive to yourself, neither remaining in mortal
things as if they were eternal, nor despising eternal things as if they
were passing. Look down on the flesh, for it is passing away; take care
of the soul, for it is something immortal. Understand yourself with
all exactness, that you may know what gift to apportion to each—

for the flesh nourishment and coverings, and for the soul doctrines of piety, education in courtesy, training in virtue, correction of passions. Do not fatten the body excessively and do not seek a lot of flesh. For since "the flesh lusts against the spirit and the spirit against the flesh" [Gal 5.17], and these are opposite to each other, see that you do not add to the flesh and grant great power to what is inferior. For as in the turning of scales, if you weigh down one side you truly make the opposite side lighter, so also with body and soul, the increase of one necessarily produces a decrease in the other. For when the body enjoys well-being and becomes heavy through much fleshiness, the mind is necessarily inactive and slack in its proper activity; but when the soul is in good condition and through care of its own goods is raised up toward its proper greatness, following this the state of the body withers.

4   The same precept is both useful to the sick and very appropriate to the healthy. In regard to the sick, physicians recommend to the ill to be attentive to themselves and to disregard none of the things heard to bring healing. Likewise also the Word, a physician for our souls, thoroughly cures the soul afflicted by sin through this small aid. Be attentive, then, to yourself, that you may also receive the aid of healing proportionate to your offense. If the sin is great and severe, you need many confessions, bitter tears, earnestness in vigils, continual fasting. If the transgression is light and tolerable, let the repentance be equal to it. Only be attentive to yourself, that you may recognize the strength and illness of your soul. For many through lack of attention get great and incurable illnesses, and they do not themselves know that they are ill. Great is the usefulness of this precept also for strength in deeds; thus the same thing both heals the sick and makes perfect the healthy.

For each of us who are disciples of the Word is a servant in one particular activity appointed to us among those in accord with the Gospel. For in the great house of the church there are not only vessels of every kind, gold and silver and wood and earthenware

[2 Tim 2.20], but also skills of all kinds. For the house of God, which is the church of the living God [1 Tim 3.15] has hunters, travelers, architects, builders, farmers, shepherds, athletes, soldiers. This brief word is appropriate to all of them, producing in each both exactitude of action and eagerness of will. You are a hunter sent by the Lord, who said, "Behold, I am sending many hunters, and they will hunt them atop every mountain" [Jer 16.16]. Be carefully attentive to yourself, lest perhaps the prey flee from you, that being caught by the word of truth those made savage by evil may be led to the Savior. You are a traveler like the one who prayed, "Make straight my steps" [Ps 118.133]. Be attentive to yourself, lest you turn aside from the road, lest you turn away to the right or left [cf. Deut 17.20]; go on the royal road. Let the architect firmly lay the foundation of faith, which is Christ Jesus. Let the builder watch what he builds on it, not wood, not hay, not straw, but gold, silver, precious stones [1 Cor 3.10]. Shepherd, be attentive lest any of your duties as a shepherd escape your notice. And what are these? Lead back the stray, bind up the broken, heal the sick. Farmer, dig around the unfruitful fig tree and place there what will help its fruitfulness. Soldier, share in sufferings for the Gospel, fight the good fight against the spirits of evil, against the passions of the flesh, take up all the full armor of the Spirit. Do not be entangled in the business of life, that you may please the one who has made you a soldier [2 Tim 2.4]. Athlete, be attentive to yourself, lest perhaps you transgress any of the athletic rules. For nobody is crowned if he does not strive lawfully [2 Tim 2.5]. Imitate Paul, and run, and wrestle, and box; and like a good boxer, keep the gaze of your soul undistracted. Shield your vital organs by putting your hands in front of them; let your eye look intently toward your opponent. In the race, stretch forward to what lies ahead. Run so that you may obtain. In wrestling, struggle against the invisible opponents. Such a one the Word wishes you to be throughout your life, not frightened, nor lying idle, but soberly and vigilantly watching over yourself.

5   I lack the time to describe in full the pursuits of those who work together in the Gospel of Christ, and the power of this commandment, how it is well suited to all. Be attentive to yourself; be sober, able to deliberate, protective of present things, cautious toward things to come. Do not through laziness give up what is already present, and do not take for granted the enjoyment of things that do not exist, or things that perhaps will not exist, as if they were in your hands. Does not this infirmity naturally exist in the young, who having frivolously expansive minds regard things hoped for as already present? For when they have time during the day, or in the quiet of night, they invent for themselves insubstantial fantasies and are carried along by them through the agility of the mind, imagining an illustrious life, a brilliant marriage, happiness in their children, a long old age, honor from all. Though the things they hope for can nowhere be actualized, they become unduly inflated toward the greatest of human attainments. Acquiring large and beautiful houses filled with all kinds of treasures, they encompass land, as much as the vanity of their thoughts can appropriate from the whole creation. Thereupon they enclose wealth in storehouses of vanity. To these things they add cattle, a crowd of household slaves surpassing number, civic authority, sovereignty over nations, military commands, wars, triumphs, kingship itself. As all these things happen through the empty invention of the mind, through much folly they seem to enjoy the things they hope for as already present and lying at their feet. This weakness belongs to a lazy and indifferent soul, to see dream visions while the body is awake. Therefore the Word compresses this frivolous expansion of the mind and inflammation of the thoughts, and like a kind of bridle halting the unstable mind, it mandates this great and wise precept. To yourself be attentive, it says, not taking nonexistent things for granted, but manage present things advantageously with a view to what takes place.

Yet I believe that the Legislator also uses this exhortation to remove a habitual passion. Since it is easy for each of us to meddle in things belonging to others rather than examining things belonging to ourselves, that we may not suffer from this it says, stop busying yourself with these dangerous evils. Do not spend time through thoughts scrutinizing the weakness that belongs to another, but be attentive to yourself, that is, turn the eye of your soul to inquire about things that belong to you. For many, according to the word of the Lord, who observe well the twig in the eye of their brother, do not look at the beam in their own eye [Mt 7.3]. Therefore do not cease examining yourself closely, to see whether life proceeds for you according to the commandments; but do not look around at things outside yourself in case perhaps you can find some fault, like that stern and boastful Pharisee, who having set himself up as just also greatly despised the publican [cf. Lk 18.11]. Do not cease examining yourself as to whether you have sinned somehow in thought, whether somehow your tongue has slipped, running ahead of your mind, whether in the works of your hands you have done something inadvisable. And if you find in your own life many sins (and you will surely find some, being human), say the words of the publican, "O God, be gracious to me, the sinner" [Lk 18.13].

Be attentive to yourself. This word is for you also when you are brilliantly successful, and all of your life is flowing like a stream. It is useful in protecting you as a kind of good adviser bringing a reminder of things human. And of course also when hard pressed by circumstances, on occasion you can sing it in your heart, so that you are not lifted up by conceit to excessive pretension, nor do you give in to ignoble thoughts, falling into despair. Are you proud of wealth? And do you have grand thoughts about your ancestors? And do you exult in your homeland and bodily beauty and the honors given you by all? Be attentive to yourself, mindful that you are mortal, that "you are earth, and to earth you will return" [Gen 3.19]. Look around, examining those of like eminence before you. Where are those who possessed civil authority? Where are the unconquerable orators? Where are the leaders of public assemblies, the brilliant horse breeders, the generals, the governors, the despots? Are they not all dust? Are they not all legend? Are not the memorials of their lives a few bones? Stoop and look into the tombs to see if you can distinguish which is the slave and which is the master, which is the poor one and which is the rich. Distinguish, if such power is yours, the captive from the king, the strong from the weak, the attractive from the mis-shapen. So having remembered your nature you will not then be conceited. And you will remember yourself if you are attentive to yourself.

6   Again, are you someone low born and obscure, a poor person born of the poor, without home or country, sick, in need every day, trembling at those in power, cowering before all because of your lowly life? "For one who is poor," Scripture says, "is not subjected to threats" [Prov 13.8]. Therefore do not despair of yourself because nothing enviable belongs to you in your present circumstances, do not renounce the hope of all good; but lift up your soul toward the good things made present to you already by God, and toward the things laid up in store through his promise for later. First, then, you are a human being, the only one of the animals formed by God [cf. Gen 2.7]. Is this not enough to be reasonable grounds for the most exalted joy, that you have been entirely formed by the very hands of God who has made all things? That since you have come into being according to the image of the Creator you can ascend quickly toward equality of honor with the angels through good conduct? You have been given an intellectual soul, through which you comprehend God, you perceive by thought the nature of beings, you pluck the sweetest fruit of wisdom. All the land animals, domesticated and wild, and all those living in water, and all those that fly through the air, belong to you as slaves and are subject to you. Further, have you not invented arts, and built cities, and devised all the things per-taining to necessity and luxury? Are not the oceans passable for you through reason? Do not earth and sea serve your life? Do not air and sky and dancing stars disclose to you their pattern? Why then are you downcast because your horse does not have a silver-mounted bridle? Yet you have the sun carrying its torch for you in a swift race through

the whole day. You do not have the luster of silver and gold, but you have the moon with its limitless light shining around you. You have not mounted a chariot inlaid with gold, but you have feet as a vehicle proper and adapted by nature to yourself. Therefore, why do you call happy one who has a fat purse but needs the feet of others to move around? You do not lie on a bed of ivory [cf. Am 6.4], but you have the earth which is more valuable than great amounts of ivory, and your rest upon it is sweet, sleep comes quickly and is free from anxiety. You do not lie beneath a gilded roof, but you have the sky glittering all around with the inexpressible beauty of the stars. Now these are human things, but those of which we will now speak are still greater. These things are for your sake: God present among human beings, the distribution of the Holy Spirit, the destruction of death, the hope of resurrection, divine ordinances perfecting your life, the journey toward God through the commandments; the kingdom of heaven is ready and crowns of righteousness are prepared for one who has not fled from labors on behalf of virtue.

7   If you are attentive to yourself, you will discover these things about yourself and still more, and you will enjoy the things present and will not be downcast about what you lack. This precept will be a great help if you are mindful of it on all occasions. For instance, has anger gained mastery over your thoughts, and have you been carried away by temper toward inappropriate words and savage, beast-like actions? If you were attentive to yourself, you would curb your temper like some disobedient and refractory colt, striking it with a blow of reason as if by a lash. You would also control your tongue, and you would not lay hands on the one provoking you. Again, evil desires madden the soul, casting you into incontinent and licentious impulses. If you were attentive to yourself and remembered that for you this present enjoyment will result in a bitter end, and this tickling, which through pleasure has now come about in your body, will bring forth the venomous worm punishing us forever in hell, and the burning of the flesh will become mother

of eternal fire, immediately the pleasures will be gone and banished. A certain wondrous inner calm and quiet in the soul will also come into being, as when the noise of undisciplined servant girls becomes silent through the entrance of a discreet lady. Therefore be attentive to yourself, and know that the rational part of the soul is also intelligent, but the passionate part is also irrational. And the one exists by nature to rule, while the other exists to obey reason and be persuaded by it. So do not ever allow your mind, reduced to utter slavery, to become a slave of the passions; moreover, do not yield to the passions struggling against reason and let them transfer to themselves the rule of the soul.

The exact comprehension of yourself also provides entirely sufficient guidance toward the concept of God. For if you are attentive to yourself, you will not need to trace your understanding of the Fashioner from the structure of the universe, but in yourself, as if in a kind of small ordered world, you will see the great wisdom of the Creator. Understand that God is incorporeal from the incorporeal soul existing in you, not circumscribed by place; since neither as a matter of principle does your mind spend its life in a place, but through its conjunction with the body it comes to be in a place. You believe God to be invisible in understanding your own soul, since it also is ungraspable with bodily eyes, for it is colorless, it is without shape, and it has not been encompassed by any bodily characteristic, but it is recognized only from its energies. So nor should you investigate God by understanding through the eyes, but supporting faith by reason, have spiritual understanding about him. Marvel at the Creator's work, how the power of your soul has been bound together with the body, so that penetrating to its extremities it leads the many separate limbs and organs to one convergence and sharing of life. Examine what power from the soul is given to the flesh, what sympathy is given back to the soul by the flesh; how the body receives life from the soul, and the soul receives pain from the body. Examine where you have stored away the things you have learned; why the addition of things that have come later does not overshadow the knowledge of things retained, but without confusion you keep your memories distinct, inscribed on the directive faculty of the soul as if on a bronze slab, guarded closely. Examine how as the soul slips gradually toward the passions of the flesh its own beauty is destroyed; and how again cleansed from the shame of evil, through virtue it ascends quickly toward the likeness of the Creator.

8   If you like, after your contemplation of the soul be attentive also to the structure of the body and marvel at how appropriate a dwelling for the rational soul the sovereign Fashioner has created. He has made the human being alone of the animals upright, that from your very form you may see that your life is akin to that on high; for all the quadrupeds are bent down toward their stomachs, while the human being is prepared to look up toward heaven, so as not to be devoted to the stomach or to the passions below the stomach but to direct his whole desire toward the journey on high. Then God placed the head at the top, locating in it the most valuable of the senses. There sight, and hearing, and taste, and smell have been established, all near each other. And although confined in a small space, none of them impedes the activity of its neighbor. The eyes have laid hold of the highest lookout point so that nothing blocks their view of the body's parts, but placed under the small projection of the eyebrows, they reach out from the prominence above in a direct line. Again, the hearing is not directed straight, but by a spiral-shaped pathway it takes hold of the noises in the air. This indeed exhibits the highest wisdom, enabling sound to pass though unhindered, or rather be led in, bending around the twists, while nothing from outside that accidentally falls in can be a hindrance to the auditory perception. Examine closely the nature of the tongue, how it is tender and nimble and is sufficient by its varied movement for every need of speech. Teeth, also organs of speech, provide strong resistance to the tongue and at the same time also take care of food, some cutting it and others grinding it. And so when you have traversed all things with suitable reflection on each, and have observed carefully

how air is drawn in through breath, how warmth is kept around the heart, and the organs of digestion, and the channels of blood, from all these you will perceive the unsearchable wisdom of the Creator [Rom 11.33]. So you will also say to him with the prophet, "Your knowledge from myself has become wonderful" [Ps 138.6]. Therefore be attentive to yourself, that you may be attentive to God, to whom be glory and dominion unto the ages. Amen.

Letter 233, to Bishop Amphilochius, Who Has Asked a Question

1   I know indeed that I myself have heard this, and I am acquainted with the structure of human beings. What, then, shall we say regarding these matters? That the mind is good and in it we have that which is according to the image of the Creator, and the activity of the mind is good, and that as it is always in motion it often forms images of nonexistent things as if they existed, yet it often heads straight toward the truth. But, according to our understanding as believers in God, a twofold power has emerged along with it. One aspect is wicked and from the demons and draws us with them toward our own apostasy, while the other is more divine and good and leads us toward the likeness of God. So when the mind remains in itself it perceives small things commensurate with itself, but when it gives itself to the deceivers it obliterates its proper faculty of judgment and meets with strange imaginings. Then indeed it does not regard wood as wood but as God, and does not consider gold to be money but an object of worship. But if it turns toward the more divine side and receives the gifts of the Spirit, then it becomes able to grasp the more divine realities as far as is commensurate with its own nature. Accordingly, there are, as it were, three conditions of life, and an equal number of activities of our mind. For when our pursuits are wicked, clearly the movements of our mind are also wicked, such as adultery, theft, idolatry, slander, strife, bad temper, intrigue, arrogance, and the things that the apostle Paul has numbered among the works of the flesh. In the middle

is a certain activity of the soul involving nothing that is either condemned or commended, such as acquiring the professional skills.
Indeed, these are even said to be in the middle, which in itself
inclines neither toward virtue nor toward evil. For what sorts of
evils are in the skills of the pilot or the physician? Yet of course neither are they virtues in themselves, but through the free choice of
those who use them they incline toward the side of one of the two
opposites. Yet the mind commingled with the divinity of the Spirit
already beholds the greatest visions and perceives the beauties of
God, yet only as far as the gift allows and as its own structure can
receive.

2   So, dismissing their dialectical questions, not wickedly but
devoutly, let them closely examine the truth. The mind's faculty of
judgment has been given to us for the comprehension of the truth.
But our God is the truth itself. So first of all our mind is to know our
God, but to know him as much as the infinitely great can be perceived by the very small. For although the eyes have been assigned to
the comprehension of visible things, they cannot now bring into
their view all that is visible. For the eye cannot encompass the hemi-
sphere of the sky in one glance. Rather, while a visual representation
surrounds us, in truth many things in it, not to say all, are unknown
to us: the nature of the stars, their greatness, their distances, movements, conjunctions, separations, their other qualities, the substance
itself of the firmament, the depth from the concave circumference
to the convex outer surface.[1] Yet still we would not say that the sky is
invisible because of the things unknown to us, but we consider it visible because of our modest comprehension of it. So indeed it is with

[1]Basil explains this in *On the Six Days of Creation* 3.4, in a comment on Gen 1.6–7:
"And God said, 'Let there be a dome in the midst of the waters, and let it separate the
waters....' So God made the dome and separated the waters that were under the dome
from the waters that were above the dome." Basil responds to a critic of the biblical
creation account who asks how water could stay above the dome instead of pouring
down its curved sides. He answers that there must be a bowl atop the dome's outer
surface to hold the water.

God. If the mind is misled by demons, it will worship idols or be turned aside toward some other form of impiety. But if it has opened itself to the assistance of the Spirit, it will perceive the truth and know God. But it will know, as the apostle says, in part; but in the life after this, more perfectly. "For when what is more perfect comes, what is in part will come to an end" [1 Cor 13.10]. So indeed the mind's faculty of judgment is good and has been given for a useful purpose, the comprehension of God, yet it acts to the extent of its capacity.

Long Rules, Selections

QUESTION 1. On ranking and sequence in the commandments of the Lord.

Since the Lord has given us the authorization to ask questions, first of all we must be taught whether there is a certain ranking and sequence in the commandments of God, so that one is first, another is second, and so on; or if they all belong with each other, and as all are equal in honor to each other, bring us safely to the goal, as if indeed they form a circle and we can make a beginning wherever we like.

ANSWER. Your question is an old one and long ago was stated in the Gospels, when the lawyer came to the Lord and said, "Teacher, what is the first commandment in the law?" And the Lord answered, "You shall love the Lord your God with all your heart, and with all your soul, and with all your strength, and with all your mind. This is the first and great commandment. The second is like it: You shall love your neighbor as yourself" [Mt 22.36–39]. Therefore the Lord himself provided the ranking of his own commandments, establishing as first and greatest the commandment about love for God; and second in rank and like the first, or rather as a fulfillment of the previous one and dependent on it, the commandment about love for neighbor. So from what has been said and from other such sayings presented in the divinely inspired Scriptures, one understands the ranking and sequence in all the commandments of the Lord.

QUESTION 2. On the love toward God and that in accord with nature there is in human beings an inclination and impulse toward the Lord's commandment.

Therefore, first discuss the love of God with us. For we have heard that it is necessary to love, but we seek to learn further how this may be successfully accomplished.

ANSWER. 1 Love toward God is not taught. For neither have we learned from another to rejoice in light and to seek after life, nor did another teach us to love those who gave birth to us or raised us. Even so, then, or indeed to a much greater extent, instruction in yearning for the divine does not come from outside; but simultaneously with the fashioning of the living creature, I mean the human being, a certain seed-like principle was implanted within us that contained by nature the starting point of our appropriation of love as our own. Having received this seed, let us cultivate it with diligence at the school of God's commandments and nurture it with skill. And having grown, it is brought to perfection by the grace of God. Therefore also, since we approve your zeal as necessary to the purpose, as God grants and as you provide assistance to us by your prayers, according to the power given us through the Spirit we will hasten zealously to awaken the spark of divine love hidden within you. Yet it is necessary to know that though this is but one virtue, by its power it brings into action and attains every commandment. "For the one who loves me," says the Lord, "will keep my commandments" [Jn 14.23]; and again, "On these two commandments hang all the law and the prophets" [Mt 22.40]. We will not now attempt to discuss the whole subject with precision (for then without knowing it we would include in this section a discussion of everything about the commandments), but as is fitting for us and pertains to the present purpose, we will remind you of the love we owe to God.

But let me note first regarding all the commandments given us by God, that from him we have also received beforehand the power to practice them, so that we might neither be displeased as if something newly invented were demanded of us, nor exalt ourselves as if we contributed something more than we had been given. Through these powers, acting rightly and appropriately, we devoutly accomplish a life according to virtue; but when we corrupt their activity, we are carried down toward evil. And evil is defined in this way, as the wicked use, indeed against a commandment of God, of the powers given us by God for good. So indeed likewise the virtue sought by God is their use with a good conscience according to a commandment of God. And since this is so, we will say the same also about love.

Accordingly, having received a commandment to love God, we have the power to love, which was placed in us as a foundation simultaneously with our first fashioning. And the proof of this does not come from outside us, but anyone can perceive it by himself and in himself. For by nature we are desirous of beautiful things, though most certainly different things appear beautiful to different people. We have affection for what is close and akin to us without being taught, and we are willingly filled with all good will toward our benefactors. What, then, is more wondrous than divine beauty? What thought is more pleasant than that of the magnificence of God? What kind of yearning of the soul is so piercing and unbearable as that brought forth by God in the soul purified from all evil, and which from an authentic and true disposition says, "I am wounded by love" [Song 2.5]? The lightning flashes of the divine beauty are absolutely unutterable and ineffable; speech cannot convey them; the ear cannot receive them. The morning star's rays, and the moon's brightness, and the sun's light, all these are unworthy to be mentioned in comparison to that glory, and are found greatly wanting as analogies to the true light. They are more distant from the divine beauty than the depth of night and moonless gloom are from the pure light of noonday. This beauty is not contemplated by fleshly eyes but is grasped by the soul alone and the mind. If at any time it shined upon the saints, it also left behind in them the unbearable pain of yearning. They reached forth from themselves toward the life beyond, saying, "Woe is me that my sojourning is prolonged" [Ps 120.5], "When will I come and appear before the face of God?" [Ps 42.2], and, "It would be far better to be dissolved and be with Christ" [Phil 1.23], and, "My soul has thirsted for the strong, living God" [Ps 42.2]; and, "Lord, now let your servant depart" [Lk 2.29]. Being oppressed in this life as in a prison, they found it hard to hold back their desires as the divine yearning touched their souls. They at least, because they longed insatiably for contemplation of divine beauty, prayed that their contemplation of the delight of the Lord would be co-extensive with the whole of eternal life. So then, human beings by nature are desirous of beautiful things; but the good is in the proper sense beautiful and beloved. Now, God is the good, and all things long after good; hence all things long after God.

2   So good action arising from free choice is indeed also present in us by nature, for those at least who have not distorted their reason by wickedness. Therefore, the obligation of love toward God is demanded of us as a necessity, whose lack in the soul is of all evils the most unendurable poverty. For estrangement and turning away from God are more unbearable than the punishments expected in hell, and more oppressive to the one suffering than the deprivation of light is to the eye, even if no pain is added to it, or than the deprivation of life is to a living creature. And if indeed affection exists by nature in those born toward those who have borne them—and clearly this is the condition of the nonrational animals, and is the disposition of human beings from the earliest age toward their mothers—let us not be shown as more irrational than infants, or more savage than wild beasts, being without affection and estranged from the one who created us. Even if we did not know from his goodness of what sort he is, from the sole fact that we have been brought into being by him, we owe him exceeding love and affection, and ought to hold to a continual remembrance of him, as infants do of their mothers.

Moreover, a benefactor is by nature loved very strongly. And this is not a property of human beings alone, but indeed, all living creatures feel close friendship toward those who have given them something good. "The ox," says Scripture, "knows its owner, and the donkey its master's feeding-trough." May the words that follow be far from being said about us: "But Israel did not know me, and my people did not understand" [Is 1.3]. As for the dog, and many other such animals, what indeed need be said of the good will they show toward those who raise them? But if by nature we have good will and affection toward our benefactors, and we patiently endure every labor to repay past favors, what language can be worthy to attain to the gifts of God? They are so great in multitude as to be beyond counting; and so great is the magnitude of each, that even one would suffice to make us responsible to offer all our thankfulness to the giver. Therefore I will pass over some gifts which, though they are in themselves of surpassing greatness and grace, are yet outshone by the greater gifts, as stars are outshone by the sun's rays, though in themselves they produce a dimmer light. For there is no leisure to leave aside the surpassingly great gifts and measure from the lesser ones the goodness of the Benefactor.

3   Accordingly, let us be silent about the rising of the sun, the phases of the moon, variations in air temperature, the changing of seasons, water from the clouds and other water from the earth, the sea itself, the whole earth, the earth's produce, the creatures living in the waters, the species in the air, the myriads of different animals, all appointed for service to our life. But there is that which one neither wishes to pass over nor can, and to be silent about this gift is, at least for the healthy mind and reason, entirely inconceivable, but one is most incapable of saying anything worthy. God created the human being according to the image and likeness of God, and made him worthy of knowledge of himself, and equipped him with reason in contrast to the animals, and granted that he take delight in the inconceivable beauties of paradise, and appointed him ruler of all things

on earth. Then he was outwitted by the serpent and fell into sin, and through sin into death, and the evils attendant on this, yet God did not overlook him. First he gave the law as a help, appointed angels to guard and care for him, sent prophets to reprove evil and teach virtue, thwarted the impulse toward evil by threats, awakened eagerness for good things by promises, often revealed the outcome of good and evil in different persons, judging them in advance as a warning for others. God continued in all these and similar benefactions and did not turn away in response to our disobedience. For we were not sent away, dismissed from the goodness of the Master, nor did we thwart his love for us, as we insulted the Benefactor by insensibility to the honors given us. Rather, we were recalled from death and given life again by our Lord Jesus Christ himself. In this also the way the gift was bestowed involves a greater wonder: "Being in the form of God, he did not regard equality with God as a thing to be grasped, but emptied himself, taking the form of a slave" [Phil 2.6–7].

4   He bore our weaknesses and carried our diseases and was wounded for us, that by his bruises we might be healed [Is 53.4–5]; and he redeemed us from the curse, becoming a curse for us [Gal 3.13], and submitted to the most dishonorable death, that he might bring us back to the glorious life. And he was not satisfied merely to give life to the dead, but he also gave them the honor of divinity, and prepared eternal rest, which surpasses every human thought in the greatness of its joy. What, then, shall we give to the Lord in return for all the good things that have been given to us? He is so good that he does not demand anything in exchange, but it suffices him merely to be loved by those to whom he has given gifts.

Whenever I come to think of all these things, if I may speak of my own feelings, I fall into a certain shuddering and alienation of mind through fear, lest ever through inattention of mind, or occupation with empty concerns, in falling away from the love of God I become a reproach to Christ. For he who now deceives us, and who endeavors by contrivance through worldly enticements to produce in us forgetfulness of our benefactor, who rushes against us for the ruin of our souls and tramples upon us, will then, as a reproach, bring before the Lord our contempt and boast of our disobedience and apostasy. He in fact neither created us nor died for us, but all the same he had us as his followers in disobedience and neglect of the commandments of God. This reproach against the Lord, and this boast of the enemy, appear more oppressive to me than the punishments in hell, because we give the enemy of Christ material for boasting and a starting point from which to rise up against him who died for us and rose again. Because of this also we are most exceedingly indebted to the Lord, as it is written. And concerning the love of God, this is as much as we will say. For my purpose, as I said, is not to say everything, for that is impossible, but to produce in your souls a brief reminder of the main points, so as always to awaken in them the divine yearning.

QUESTION 3. Concerning love of neighbor.

It would make sense now to consider the commandment that comes second both in order and importance.

ANSWER. Now then, the law cultivates and nurtures the powers implanted in us as seeds, as we have said in our previous discourses; and since we have been ordered to love our neighbor as ourselves, let us examine whether we also have received from God the power to fulfill this commandment. Who, then, does not know that the human being is a tame and communal animal, and is neither solitary nor savage? For nothing is so proper to our nature as to share our lives with each other, and to need each other, and to love our own kind. As, therefore, the Lord himself granted us to receive the seeds beforehand, in accord with this he also seeks after the fruits, saying, "A new commandment I give you, that you love one another" [Jn 13.34]. And as he wished to arouse our soul toward this commandment, he did not demand in return as proof from his disciples miracles and extraordinary powers, though indeed he also enabled them to do these things in the Holy Spirit. But what does he say? "By this all will know that you are my disciples, if you have love for one another" [Jn 13.35]. And he completely joins together these commandments, so that the good action done for the neighbor is transferred to himself. "For I was hungry," he says, "and you gave me food" [Mt 25.35], and what follows. Then he adds, "Whoever has done it to one of the least of these my brothers, has done it to me" [Mt 25.40].

Therefore, through the first commandment, the second also is successfully accomplished, while through the second one returns again to the first. One who loves the Lord consequently also loves the neighbor. "For he who loves me," says the Lord, "will keep my commandments" [Jn 14.23]. "And this," he says, "is my commandment, that you love one another, even as I have loved you" [Jn 15.12]. And again, one who loves the neighbor fulfills love for God, who himself accepts the gift as given to himself. Therefore, the faithful servant of God Moses showed such great love for his brothers, as indeed to wish to have his name erased from the book of God, where it had been written, if the people's sin was not forgiven [Ex 32.32]. And Paul dared to pray to be accursed from Christ on behalf of his brothers of the same race according to the flesh, wishing in imitation of Christ to give himself in exchange for the salvation of all [Rom 9.3]. Yet at the same time he knew that it was impossible to be estranged from God through his having rejected God's favor out of love for God and for the sake of the greatest of commandments, and that because of this he was about to receive in return many times more than he had given. The things we have said provide sufficient proof that in fact the saints were first to arrive at this measure of love for their neighbor.

QUESTION 4. Concerning fear of God.

ANSWER. To those, then, who are just now being introduced to piety, the elementary teaching of fear is more useful, according to the advice of the most wise Solomon, who says, "The fear of the Lord is the beginning of wisdom" [Prov 1.7]. But you who have passed beyond infancy in Christ and no longer need milk, but are able to be perfected in the inner self by the solid food of teachings, have need of the more central commandments, in which the whole truth of love in Christ is successfully put into practice. Yet quite clearly you must be on guard, lest ever the abundance of God's gifts become for you a cause of heavier condemnation, should you become ungrateful toward your Benefactor. "For of those," it says, "to whom much is entrusted, greater things will be required" [Lk 12.48].

QUESTION 7. Concerning the necessity that those who with common purpose aim to be well pleasing to God live together, and that to live as a solitary is difficult and dangerous.

Since, then, your discourse has convinced us that it is dangerous to live with those who have contempt for the commandments of the Lord, accordingly it is fitting that we learn if it is necessary for one who has withdrawn from them to live alone by himself, or to live together with brothers of common purpose who also choose the same aim of piety.

ANSWER. 1 For many reasons I consider spending life with many in the same place to be more useful. First, this is because no one of us is self-sufficient for our own bodily needs, but in the procurement of necessities we need each other. For indeed the foot has power in one regard, but in another is lacking, and without the cooperation of the other limbs finds that it is neither able nor sufficient in itself to continue in its own activity, nor does it have a remedy to bring support in what is lacking. Likewise in the solitary life even what is present to us becomes useless, and what is wanting is irremediable, since God the Fashioner determined that we would need one another, as indeed it is written [Eccl 13.20], so that we also would be bound together with each other. Moreover, apart from this consideration, the principle of

Christ's love does not direct each to aim at what is proper to himself. "For love," it says, "does not seek its own" [1 Cor 13.5]. But the solitary life has one aim, to serve the needs proper to each. But it is clear beforehand that this is in conflict with the law of love, which the apostle Paul fulfilled, seeking what was advantageous not to himself but to many others, that they might be saved [1 Cor 10.33].

Moreover, in seclusion each will not easily recognize his own defect, since he will not have anyone to reprove him and with meekness and compassion correct him. For a reproof even from an enemy may often produce a desire for healing in the prudent; but healing of sin is accomplished successfully and with knowledge by one who loves sincerely. "For one who loves," it says, "disciplines with care" [Prov 13.24]. For one who is alone, such a person is difficult to find, unless they were united in life beforehand; therefore, what has been said happens to him: "Woe to one who is alone, since if he falls there is no one to raise him up" [Eccl 4.10].

Besides, most of the commandments are easily fulfilled by many people in one place, but for one this is no longer the case, for the practice of one commandment hinders another. For instance, when visiting the sick one cannot welcome the stranger; and when distributing and sharing necessities, especially if providing these services for a long time, the zeal for other works is hindered. So for this cause the commandment that is greatest and most important for salvation is neglected, since one is neither feeding the hungry, nor clothing the naked. Who, then, would prefer the idle and fruitless life to that which is fruitful and fulfills the commandments of the Lord?

2   And if indeed we all, who share in the one hope of our calling [Eph 4.4], are one body, having Christ as head, and are each members of one another [1 Cor 12.12], if we are not fitted together in the Holy Spirit to join in concord into one body, but each of us chooses the solitary life, we will not serve the common good with coordinated planning according to God's good pleasure, but fulfill our own passion for self-indulgence. When we are split off and divided, how

can we preserve the relationship and service of the members to each other, or our submission toward our head, that is Christ? For one cannot rejoice with one who rejoices or suffer with one who suffers when living separately, since in all likelihood one will not be able to know each neighbor's concerns. Therefore indeed, as one is not sufficient to receive all the spiritual gifts, but the additional help of the Spirit is given in proportion to the faith of each [Rom 12.6], in community life the gift proper to each becomes common to those living together. "For to one is given a word of wisdom, and to another a word of knowledge, to another faith, to another prophesy, to another gifts of healing," and so on [1 Cor 12.8–10]; the one who receives each of these has it no more for his own sake than for the sake of others. Consequently, in community life the activity of the Holy Spirit in one person must pass to everyone together. So the one living by himself perhaps has one gift, and he makes it useless because it is uncultivated, buried in the earth within himself. This indeed involves great danger, as all see who have read the Gospels. But when many live together, each indeed both enjoys his own gift, multiplying it through sharing, and profits from the gifts of others as his own.

3   Life together in one place also has many benefits, which indeed cannot all easily be numbered. For preserving the good things given us by God it is more useful than the solitary life, as also for guarding against the plots of the enemy that come from outside. The one awakened by those who have kept watch is more secure, if ever it should happen that one is drowsy with the sleep that leads to death. Regarding this, David has taught us to pray that it not happen to us, saying, "Illumine my eyes, lest ever I sleep in death" [Ps 13.3]. For the sinner, withdrawal from sin is easier, since he is turned around by the condemnation coming from many in concord, so that this saying is appropriate to him: "This rebuke is enough for such a person, which is given by many" [2 Cor 2.6]. The righteous finds great assurance in the evaluation of many and their approval of his work. For if by the mouths of two or three witnesses every word will be established, very

clearly the one accomplishing the good work will be more securely confirmed by the testimony of many. But other dangers befall the solitary life besides those of which we have spoken. The first and greatest is self-satisfaction. For having nobody who will be able to evaluate his work, one thinks he has attained perfection in the commandments. So, compelled by habit, he always remains untrained, and he neither comes to know his own deficiencies nor recognizes the progress in his works, since he has removed himself from all opportunities to practice the commandments.

4   For how will he manifest his humility, since he has nobody beside whom he can show himself more humble? How will he manifest his compassion, since he has cut himself off from the community of many? How will he train himself in longsuffering when nobody opposes his wishes? But if one says the teaching of the divine Scriptures is sufficient for the correction of his conduct, he is like one who has learned carpentry but has never done any carpentry, and one who has been taught metal work but has never chosen to put what he has learned into practice. To him the apostle would say, "It is not the hearers of the law who are righteous before God, but the doers of the law will be made righteous" [Rom 2.13]. For see, the Lord in exceeding compassion did not find it sufficient to teach only by word, but so as to transmit to us precisely and visibly the pattern of humility in the perfection of love, he himself girded himself and washed the feet of the disciples. Whom, then, will you wash? Whom will you serve? In relation to whom will you be the last, you who spend life by yourself? But as for that good and pleasant condition, the dwelling of brothers in one place, which the Holy Spirit compares to myrrh emitting a fragrance from the high priest's head [Ps 133.1–2], how, when dwelling in solitude, will this be accomplished? Thus it is an arena for struggle, a fragrance of progress, and continuous training and practice of the Lord's commandments when brothers dwell in one place. It has as its aim the glory of God according to the commandment of our Lord Jesus Christ, who says, "Let

your light so shine before others, that they may see your good works and glorify your Father who is in heaven" [Mt 5.16]. And it preserves the distinctive mark of the saints as narrated in the Acts, about whom it is written, "All who believed were in one place, and they had all things in common" [Acts 2.44], and again, "The whole group of those who believed were of one heart and soul, and nobody said that anything he had was his own, but to them all things were common" [Acts 4.32].

Select Bibliography

Texts

Courtonne, Yves, ed. and trans. *Saint Basile: Lettres*. 3 vols. Paris: Les Belles Lettres, 1957–66.

Migne, J. P. et al., ed. *Patrologia Graeca* 31. Paris: 1857-.

Rudberg, Stig Y. *L'homélie de Basile de Césarée sur le mot 'Observe-toi toi-même': Édition critique du texte grec et étude sur la tradition manuscrite*. Acta Universitatis Stockholmiensis, Studia Graeca Stockholmiensia 2. Stockholm: Almqvist & Wiksell, 1962.

Smets, Alexis, and Michel van Esbroeck, ed. and trans. *Basile de Césarée: Sur l'origine de l'homme*. Sources chrétiennes 160. Paris: Cerf, 1970.

Translations

Anderson, David, trans. *St Basil the Great: On the Holy Spirit*. Crestwood, NY: St Vladimir's Seminary Press, 1980.

Jackson, Blomfield, trans. *St Basil: Letters and Select Works*. Nicene and Post-Nicene Fathers, ser. 2, vol. 8. Oxford: Parker, 1895. [Now available for free on the Internet.]

Rosset, Marie-Claude. "Basile de Césarée: Dieu n'est pas l'auteur des maux," in *Dieu et le mal selon Basile de Césarée, Grégoire de Nysse, Jean Chrysostome*, Marie-Hélène Congourdeau, ed. Paris: Migne, 1997.

Wagner, M. Monica, trans. *St Basil: Ascetical Works*. Fathers of the Church 9. Washington, DC: Catholic University of America Press, 1962.

Way, Agnes Clare, trans. *St Basil: Exegetic Homilies*. Fathers of the Church 46. Washington, DC: Catholic University of America Press, 1963.

Way, Agnes Clare, trans. *St Basil: Letters*. 2 vols. Fathers of the Church 13 and 28. Washington, DC: Catholic University of America Press, 1951–55.

Studies

Aghiorgoussis, Maximos. *In the Image of God: Studies in Scripture, Theology, and Community.* Brookline, MA: Holy Cross Orthodox Press, 1998. Pp. 9–74. [The author is Metropolitan of Ainou.]

Elm, Susanna. *"Virgins of God": The Making of Asceticism in Late Antiquity.* Oxford: Oxford University Press, 1994.

Fedwick, Paul Jonathan, ed. *Basil of Caesarea: Christian, Humanist, Ascetic.* 2 vols. Toronto: Pontifical Institute of Mediaeval Studies, 1981.

Gribomont, Jean. *Saint Basile: évangile et église.* 2 vols. Spiritualité Orientale 36 and 37. Bégrolles-en-Mauges, France: Abbaye de Bellefontaine, 1984.

Harrison, Verna E. F. "Male and Female in Cappadocian Theology." *Journal of Theological Studies,* n.s. 41 (1990): 441–71.

Holman, Susan R. *The Hungry are Dying: Beggars and Bishops in Roman Cappadocia.* New York: Oxford University Press, 2001.

Holmes, Augustine. *A Life Pleasing to God: The Spirituality of the Rules of St Basil.* Cistercian Studies Series 189. Kalamazoo, MI and Spencer, MA: Cistercian Publications, 2000.

Keidel, Anne. "*Hesychia,* Prayer and Transformation in Basil of Caesarea." *Studia Patristica* 34 (2001): 110–20.

Meredith, Anthony. *The Cappadocians.* Crestwood, NY: St Vladimir's Seminary Press, 1995.

Rousseau, Philip. *Basil of Caesarea.* Berkeley: University of California Press, 1994.

Shaw, Teresa M. *The Burden of the Flesh: Fasting and Sexuality in Early Christianity.* Philadelphia: Fortress Press, 1998.

Stramara, Daniel F. "Double Monasticism in the Greek East: Fourth through Eighth Centuries." *Journal of Early Christian Studies* 6 (1998): 269–312.

ST VLADIMIR'S SEMINARY PRESS
575 Scarsdale Rd., Crestwood, New York 10707-1699
1-800-204-2665 • www.svspress.com